Table of Contents

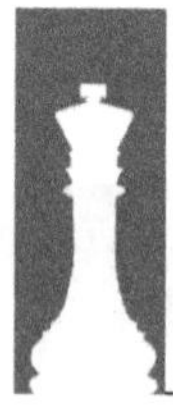

The Mandate

To:

*'...Set In Order The Things That Are Out Of Order
And Raise And Appoint Leaders In Every City.'*
- Titus 1:5

Michael Hutton-Wood Ministries
Releasing Potential
- Maximizing Destiny

House Of Judah (Praise) Ministries
&
Leaders Factory International
Raising Generational Leaders
- Impacting Nations

SIMPA:

Sceptre International Ministers & Pastors Association

MANDATE:

Equipping, Empowering, Coaching, Mentoring And Providing
Covering For Pastors, Ministers And
Leaders Across The Nations!

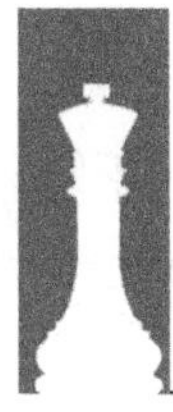# Introduction

"The thoughts of the diligent tend only to plenteousness; but of every one that is hasty only to want." (Proverbs 21:5)

Helen Hayes states the difference between achievement and success as narrated by her mother: "Achievement is the knowledge that you have studied and worked hard and done the best that is in you. Success is being praised by others, and that's nice too, but not as important or satisfying. Always aim for achievement and forget about success." Bits & Pieces, August, 1989.

God wants us to maximise our potential by being very productive to fulfil our mandate in Genesis 1:26-28. Productivity means product of activity.

In this book, we will be examining WHAT SEPARATES ACHIEVERS FROM NON-ACHIEVERS?

WHAT ARE THE DISINGUISHING FACTORS THAT MAKE ACHIEVERS OUTSTANDING AND EXTRAORDINARY IN THEIR FIELDS?

Some Of Those Factors Include:

They Reinvent themselves while others stay the same. Plan while others are playing. DESIGN THEIR SUCCESS AND

THEIR FUTURE WHILE OTHERS THINK SUCCESS IS BY DEFAULT! Study while others are sleeping. Pay now and play later. Decide while others are delaying. Step out while others stall. Pursue while others are procrastinating. Decide while others are undecided. Prepare while others are daydreaming or procrastinating. Begin while others are stalling or stagnant. Work while others are wishing and waiting for time and chance. Think while others are worrying. Worrying is the art of using your mind to magnify problems while thinking is the art of using your mind to generate and solve problems! Create or make Room to accommodate the enlargement they are expecting. Save while others are wasting. Invest while others are on a spending spree. Foolish people waste money, average people spend money but wise people invest money. Listen while others are talking. Persist while others are quitting, but winners don't quit and quitters don't win. They Never, never, never give up as Winston Churchill said.

Under-achievement is characterised by fear of commitment to success-related activities, lack of belief in one's self and avoidance of tasks that are challenging. We can achieve to any extent we aim at, "…with man this is impossible, but with God all things are possible." (Matthew 19:26). Achievers embrace challenges and take chances. In life competition is important, but satisfaction is more important. The feeling that you have done your best is more important than anything else. Our job is to keep doing our best, but it has to really be the best.

We can achieve a lot more by committing ourselves to maximising our potential, take the first step, continue taking

SECRETS
OF HIGH
ACHIEVERS

What Distinguishes Achievers from Non-Achievers

MICHAEL HUTTON-WOOD

small steps daily, and be prepared to go through the temporal pains that lead to success.

Under-achievers believe that success is based on luck and so, leave things to drift and take no personal responsibility for their progress. AVERAGE PEOPLE BELIEVE IN LUCK; ACHIEVERS BELIEVE IN THE LAW OF CAUSE AND EFFECT. Success consists of little daily efforts and failure consists of little daily neglects. Many people believe they lack the ability and resources to reach their next level of success, and prefer to remain within their comfort zone but we need to keep pressing "…toward the mark for the prize of the high calling of God in Christ Jesus" (Philippians 3:14).

INPUT DETERMINES OUTPUT! It is not reasonable to expect maximum results with minimum effort. We are the only ones that can tell whether we are putting our best into achieving our goals. "Don't settle for average. Bring your best to the moment. Then, whether it fails or succeeds, at least you know you gave all you had. We need to give the best that is in us." (Angela Bassett). In the long run average actions will yield average results. If we give a dream everything we have, we will get from it everything there is.

REMEMBER:

"When a man is no longer anxious to do better than well, he is done for." - Benjamin Haydon

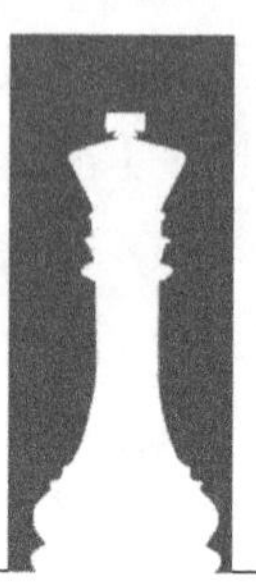

*"There Are No Limitations
To The Mind Except Those
That We Acknowledge"*

- Napoleon Hill

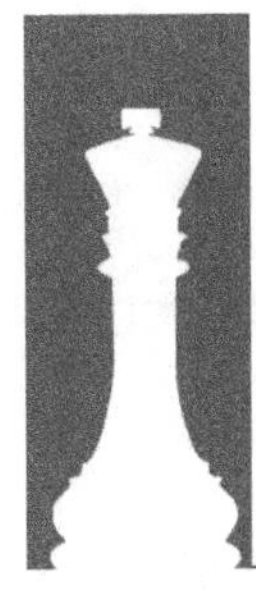

Chapter One

40 KEYS TO BECOMING A HIGH ACHIEVER

40 DAILY HABITS OF EXCEPTIONALLY SUCCESSFUL PEOPLE AND HIGH ACHIEVERS

Success breeds success. ADOPT THESE HABITS!

When you see people who are capable of achieving or accomplishing extraordinary things, you can't help but wonder, *What is it that makes them so different?*

Aliko Dangote, a <u>Nigerian</u> billionaire, who owns the <u>Dangote Group</u>, which has interests in commodities and is ranked as the richest person in Africa, made this statement: "It took me 30 years to get to where I am today. Youths of today aspire to be like me but they want to achieve it overnight. It's not going to work. To build a successful business, you must start small and dream big. In the journey of entrepreneurship, tenacity of purpose is supreme."

Who is an Achiever?

A person who achieves a high or specified level of success.

Characteristics of High Achievers

What Separates or Distinguishes Achievers (Risk-Takers From Non-Achievers (Non-Risk Takers).

Numerous studies show recurring characteristics congruent with <u>high achievers</u>. These characteristics are universally applicable for individuals, churches, departments, students, adults, marriages, relationships, organisations, Christians etc.

KNOWLEDGE IS NOT POWER; APPLIED KNOWLEDGE IS POWER [John 8:31-32]

Contrary to what we've heard in the past, Knowledge is not power; applied knowledge is power!

SUCCESS AND ACHIEVEMENTS IN LIFE ARE NOT DETERMINED JUST BY WHAT YOU HEAR or KNOW BUT WHAT YOU DO WITH WHAT YOU HEAR AND KNOW.

Joshua 1:8, NIV, *"Keep this Book of the Law always on your lips; meditate on it day and night, so that you may be careful to do everything written in it. Then you will be prosperous and successful."*

Luke 11:28, *"But he said, Yea rather, blessed, prosperous, happy, successful are they that hear the word of God, and keep (practise) it."*

1. THEY ARE GOD-SEEKERS AND GOD-CHASERS.

They Seek God, the will of God for their life and the help of the Holy Spirit. (Zechariah 4:6; 1 Samuel 2:9; Exodus 33:15;

John 1:3; Genesis 1:1-3; Proverbs 4:7; Isaiah 11:1-3; Luke 21:15)

2. THEY ARE PERSISTENT AND TENACIOUS AND DON'T TAKE NO FOR AN ANSWER.

They have the 'If I perish, I perish' attitude of Esther (Esther 4:16) and 'We are well able to take the land' attitude of Joshua and Caleb (Numbers 13:30).

They Refuse to take no for an answer. Like Isaac, you may dig one well and your enemies will fill it; go dig another till you find your own Rehoboth and go beyond Rehoboth; (Genesis 26:22) that's what high achievers do; they never quit.

Proverbs 24:10, *"If you faint in the day of adversity, your strength or your faith is small."*

"If you fail under pressure, your strength is too small." (NLT)

When you've hit a wall, it's easy to consider that as the end of the road and tend to give up. Only the most stubborn among us will persevere long enough to climb the rest of the mountain. Think of the Wright brothers trying to get people in the air. Can you imagine what their peers said? Today, we can't imagine a world without planes.

Those who say it can't be done are always interrupted by others doing it. Failure is an opportunity to start all over again but wiser.

That's why Winston Churchill said: 'Never, Never, Never Give Up.'

THE PERSISTENT ARE THOSE WHO CAN SEE THE STARS WHILE THEY ARE STILL IN THE GUTTER.

Hebrews 12:2, *"...For the joy that was set before him, Jesus endured the cross."*

3. THEY ARE EARLY-RISERS AND EARLY-SEEKERS:

They rise earlier, seek earlier, arrive earlier, start earlier, work harder, work smarter and leave later!

NO WONDER THEY ARE HIGH ACHIEVERS!

EARLY-RISERS ARE EARLY-ACHIEVERS!!

THEY ARE ALWAYS AHEAD OF SCHEDULE OR ON SCHEDULE!

"I rise before dawn and cry for help; I wait for your words" (Psalm 119:147).

"The difference between rising at five and seven o'clock in the morning, for forty years, supposing a man go to bed at the same hour at night, is nearly equivalent to the addition of ten years to a man's life." – Philip Doddridge

SLEEPING 8 HOURS A DAY IS EQUIVALENT TO SLEEPING A QUARTER OF YOUR LIFE AWAY OR WASTING A QUARTER OF YOUR LIFE i.e. 25 out of 100 years or 30 out of 120 years.

The discipline of rising early in the morning to pray or carry out important tasks has un-surpassing rewards. For many people, the ideal time to meet face to face with God is early in the morning. Jesus distinctively modelled early morning prayers whilst He was on earth.

"And rising very early in the morning, while it was still dark, he departed and went out to a desolate place, and there he prayed." - Mark 1:35

No two days are the same and you need God's help and guidance to tackle whatever each day throws at you. When you spend time praying early in the morning, committing your day to God, you will give Him a chance to breathe His life and power into your day.

EVEN GOD IS AN EARLY RISER, ACHIEVER AND EVENING WORKER!

Genesis 3:8, *"When the man and his wife heard the sound of the* Lord *God as he was walking in the garden in the cool of the day, and they hid from the* Lord *God among the trees of the garden."*

EXAMPLES OF THE SUCCESSFUL AND ACHIEVING PATRIARCHS:

Abraham rose early in the Morning (Genesis 19:27).

In Genesis 24:63, Isaac went out to meditate in the field toward evening and he lifted up his eyes and looked, and saw Rebekah...

Genesis 28:18 says, *"And Jacob rose up early in the morning"* and consecrated an altar before God ... the evening, like Isaac, who *"went out into the field to meditate at the evening".*

Psalm 63:1-2, *"O God, thou art my God; early will I seek thee: my soul thirsteth for thee, my flesh longeth for thee in a dry and thirsty land, where no water is; To see thy power and thy glory, so as I have seen thee in the sanctuary."*

Getting up early to pray and study God's word is one of the most dependable ways to have a consistent prayer life and have a word bath. Moses rose early in the morning to pray (Exodus 24:4); Samuel's parents (Hannah and Elkanah) rose up early to worship the Lord (1 Samuel 1:19); David rose up early in the morning to pray three times a day and sing seven times a day (Psalm 63; 55:17; 119:164). Jesus rose up a great while before day to a solitary place to pray (Mark1:35).

Wisdom personified and speaking through King Solomon said in Proverbs 8:17-21, *"I love them that love me; and those that seek me early shall find me. Riches and honour are with me; yea, durable riches and righteousness. My fruit is better than gold, yea, than fine gold; and my revenue than choice silver. I lead in the way of righteousness, in the midst of the paths of judgment: That I may cause those that love me to inherit substance; and I will fill their treasures."*

The devil will do everything to prevent you from rising early to meet with God or chase your dream. The Bible says in Psalm 143:8, *"Let me hear in the morning of your steadfast love, for in you I trust. Make me know the way I should go, for to you I lift my soul".*

Remember the popular saying, 'no pain, no gain'. What can be more valuable than starting the day with our heavenly Father? Early rising will increase your productivity as you will have more time to accomplish your goals for the day.

Joshua 3:1, *"And Joshua rose early in the morning; and they removed from Shittim, and came to Jordan, he and all the children of Israel, and lodged there before they passed over."*

Isaiah 33:2-3, 6, *"O Lord, be gracious unto us; we have waited for thee: be thou their arm every morning, our salvation also in the time of trouble. At the noise of the tumult the people fled; at the lifting up of thyself the nations were scattered...And wisdom and knowledge shall be the stability of thy times, and strength of salvation: the fear of the Lord is his treasure."*

Isaiah 48:17-19, 21-22, *"Thus saith the Lord, thy Redeemer, the Holy One of Israel; I am the Lord thy God which teacheth thee to profit, which leadeth thee by the way that thou shouldest go.*

O that thou hadst hearkened to my commandments! then had thy peace been as a river, and thy righteousness as the waves of the sea: Thy seed also had been as the sand, and the offspring of thy bowels like the gravel thereof; his name should not have been cut off nor destroyed from before me."

Benefit: "And they thirsted not when he led them through the deserts: he caused the waters to flow out of the rock for them: he clave the rock also, and the waters gushed out. There is no peace, saith the Lord, unto the wicked."

Psalm 32:8, *"I will instruct thee and teach thee in the way which thou shalt go: I will guide thee with mine eye."*

New Living Translation

The LORD says, *"I will guide you along the best pathway for your life. I will advise you and watch over you."*

Psalms 119:147-148, *"I prevented the dawning of the morning, and cried: I hoped in thy word. Mine eyes prevent the night watches, that I might meditate in thy word."*

Psalm 119:147-148 NIV *"I rise before dawn and cry for help; I have put my hope in your word. My eyes stay open through the watches of the night, that I may meditate on your promises."*

No wonder Martin Luther said: *"I have so much to do that I shall spend the first three hours in prayer."*

And John Bunyan said: *"He who runs from God in the morning will scarcely find Him the rest of the day."*

4. ADDICTED TO DIVINE GUIDANCE, DIVINE LEADING AND DIVINE DIRECTION i.e. THE GOD-FACTOR or DIVINE DIMENSION:

Just because you think that's the way does not mean it's the right way. When you allow God to lead you, He leads you into profit.

GOOD DOESN'T ALWAYS MEAN GOD, BETTER DOESN'T ALWAYS CONNOTE RIGHT AND URGENT DOESN'T ALWAYS MEAN IMPORTANT OR PRIORITY!

Proverbs 16:25, *"There is a way that seemeth right unto a man but the end thereof are the ways of death."*

Isaiah 48:17 & 21, *"Thus saith the LORD, thy Redeemer, the Holy One of Israel; I am the LORD thy God which teacheth thee to profit, which leadeth thee by the way that thou shouldest go...And they thirsted not when he led them through the deserts: he caused the waters to flow out of the rock for them: he clave the rock also, and the waters gushed out."*

Psalms 32:8-9, *"I will instruct thee and teach thee in the way which thou shalt go: I will guide thee with mine eye. Be ye not as the horse, or as the mule, which have no understanding: whose mouth must be held in with bit and bridle, lest they come near unto thee."*

Psalms 103:7, *"He made known his ways unto Moses, his acts unto the children of Israel."*

Philippians 2:13, NIV, *"For it is God who works in you to will and to act in order to fulfil His good purpose."*

The richest and wisest king in his day, King Solomon, speaking in Ecclesiastes 9:11 said: *"...the race is not to the swift, nor the battle to the strong, neither yet bread to the wise, nor yet riches to men of understanding, nor favour to the men of skill..."*

GOD IS AN ACCELERATOR and can speed up our progress and overall success. He will never play our part for us. We have to do the rising early in the morning, and adequately use the developed talents He has given us. After we have done our due diligence, we can prayerfully expect Him to breathe His Spirit upon our work and take it to a level that only He can.

"God is able to do exceeding abundantly above all that we ask or think, according to the power [EXPECTATION, FAITH or POWER GENERATED FROM OUR FERVENT PRAYERS] that worketh in us" (Ephesians 3:20).

When God's power works for you, no power can work or succeed against you. (Romans 8:31; Isaiah 54:15-17)

The divine dimension divided the Red Sea, guided David's stone to the head of Goliath with a deadly force; it produced thousands of meals from five loaves and two fish before the eyes of a hungry crowd.

It was the God-Factor and Divine Dimension that turned the rod of Moses (a mere stick) into a deliverance instrument, a miracle tool and a weapon of war. The divine dimension made Peter to walk on the Sea, delivered him from drowning and flattened the wall of Jericho with little or no input from the army of Israel. Sometimes God uses the nobodies to humble the somebodies.

A West African saying warns about the dangers of stubbornness and pride: "I serve a God that can crack a palm kernel with an egg just to disgrace the stone. A God that fetches water with a basket to disgrace the bucket. A God who causes fire to lick water instead of water putting out fire to defy medical science. A God that uses a stick to bring forth iron from the sea to disgrace the magnet."

Paul said: *"But God has chosen the foolish things of the world to put to shame the wise... that no flesh should glory in His presence"* (1 Corinthians 1:27-29). Are you set or proud or stubborn in your ways? *"God resists the proud, but gives grace to the humble"* (James 4:6; Proverbs 3:34; 16:18; 29:23).

Stay humble, lest you stumble. We can expect God's power to enhance our efforts, but we must first play our part, pray to God and watch Him work wonders in our lives.

"...The eyes of the LORD run to and fro throughout the whole earth, to shew Himself strong in the behalf of them whose heart is perfect toward Him..." (2 Chronicles 16:19). Seek God's face for Divine Guidance.

Let God make the supernatural out of your natural abilities.

GOD MAKES ACHIEVERS OUT OF NON-ENTITIES!

"God often uses small matches to light up great torches." – Source unknown.

Additional Benefits of early morning divine guidance can be found in Isaiah 43.

"I never know a man come to greatness or eminence who lay abed late in the morning." – Jonathan Swift

5. ARE VERY PASSIONATE ABOUT THEIR ASSIGNMENT, PURPOSE, GOALS, PURSUITS AND OBJECTIVES:

PURPOSE WITHOUT PASSION LEADS TO NOWHERE!

PASSION IS THE VEHICLE THAT VISION RIDES IN TO ARRIVE AT ITS DESTINATION.

"But since you are like lukewarm water, neither hot or cold, I will spit you out of my mouth" (Revelation 3:16)

"Passion is when you put more energy into something than is required to do it. It is more than just enthusiasm or excitement; passion is ambition that is materialised into action to put as much heart, mind, body and soul into something as is possible." – *The Urban Dictionary.*

Purpose initiates passion, but passion ignites purpose. It takes passion to make a mark in life. Whether it is playing a musical instrument, earning a qualification, winning souls for Christ or having a successful marital relationship, passion is the key to excellence. It is not the only thing that counts in life, but without it other contributors to success may be rendered ineffective.

Jesus said, *"Blessed are those who hunger and thirst for righteousness, for they will be filled"* (Matthew 5:6).

If we are not praying, tithing, giving, serving the way we should or do not see soul-winning or kingdom advancement as an urgent matter, then we lack passion for the things of God. Jesus once told His followers, *"My food is to do the will of Him who sent me and to finish His work"* (John 4:34). **Passion is contagious; if we have it, people will notice and catch it. It is like a hurricane that brings down anything that stands in its way. Purpose without passion will lead to failure. Being passionate is the only way we can express our love for whatever we do.**

We need to be passionately curious, chase our dream with passion and love the Lord with passion. Without it, it is possible to be highly skilled and talented and still end up a failure. Passionate people demonstrate commitment, intensity, devotion, dedication, discipline, diligence, determination, loyalty, focus or concentration, selflessness and excitement in whatever they do. Passion is like wild fire; it will overcome self, defeat, fear and ignore limitations. Our passion is our strength. Without it, we won't go far.

Colossians 3:23-25, NIV *"Whatever you do, work at it with all your heart, as working for the Lord, not for human masters, since you know that you will receive an inheritance from the Lord as a reward. It is the Lord Christ you are serving. Anyone who does wrong will be repaid for their wrongs, and there is no favoritism."*

And vice versa YOU ARE ONLY PERMITTED TO REAP WHAT YOU SOW NOT WHAT YOU'VE NOT SOWN.

Hebrews 11:6, *"And without faith it is impossible to please God, because anyone who comes to him must believe that he exists and that he rewards those who earnestly (passionately or diligently) seek him."*

Passion makes you burn to rim to tell others about what you saw and heard in church about Jesus and what is working for you.

Luke 24:32-34 NIV, *"They asked each other, "Were not our hearts burning within us while he talked with us on the road and opened the Scriptures to us?" They got up and returned at once to Jerusalem. There they found the Eleven and those with them, assembled together and saying, "It is true! The Lord has risen and has appeared to Simon.""*

Psalm 69:8-9, *"I am become a stranger unto my brethren, and an alien unto my mother's children. For the zeal of thine house hath eaten me up; and the reproaches (insults) of them that reproached (insulted) thee are fallen upon me."*

Receive a fresh baptism of passion in your heart now and reject every form of lukewarmness and coldness.

"Enthusiasm moves the world" – Arthur Balfour

6. ARE BOTH STARTERS AND FINISHERS

It was Jesus who said,

"He who sets his hands to the plough and looks back is not fit for the kingdom of God," (Luke 9:62)

"My meat is to do the will of Him that sent me and to finish it," (John 4:34)

7. HAVE AND MAINTAIN A ZERO TOLERANCE FOR ENTERTAINING DISCOURAGEMENT

They don't doubt in the dark what they have seen in the light!!

Worry is the darkroom in which negatives are developed.

8. THEY PREPARE FOR WHAT THEY PRAY FOR

They don't sit and wait for things to happen; they make it happen.

"Seest thou a man that is diligent in his business; he shall not stand before mean men but the noble." (Proverbs 22:29)

So, a man's audience is determined by his diligence in life.

9. THEY PLACE NO LIMITATIONS ON THEIR MIND OR WHAT THEIR MINDS CAN GENERATE AND DO.

"THERE ARE NO LIMITATIONS TO THE MIND EXCEPT THOSE THAT WE ACKNOWLEDGE." – NAPOLEON HILL

10.   THEY DON'T GIVE UP EASILY

WHEN DOUBTERS SAY 'IT CANNOT BE DONE' I ASK MYSELF, 'WHY NOT? I DON'T UNDERSTAND THAT STATEMENT; IT'S NOT IN MY VOCABULARY AND I REFUSE TO ACCEPT THAT STATEMENT BECAUSE ALL THINGS ARE POSSIBLE TO THEM THAT BELIEVE. (John 1:12)

"OUR GREATEST WEAKNESS LIES IN GIVING UP. THE MOST CERTAIN WAY TO SUCCEEED IS ALWAYS TO TRY ONE MORE TIME." — THOMAS EDISON

11.   THEY THINK AHEAD, PLAN AHEAD AND BUILD WITH GENERATIONS IN MIND i.e. are generational thinkers, planners and builders.

They Think Ahead and Plan Ahead! Failing to plan is planning to fail. They Live Today with tomorrow in mind doing tomorrow's things today; they prepare themselves and live ready to answer tomorrow's questions today. They are generational thinkers, generational planners and generational executors.

3 Kinds Of People:

i.   Those who do yesterday's things today i.e. behind time; therefore, are late in life and having to catch up. It's sad to see People who are late in life but still have no sense of urgency

ii. Those who do today's things today i.e. on time

iii. Those who do tomorrow's things today i.e. ahead of time (Joseph solved a 14-year problem ahead of time [Genesis 41]; Daniel recalled, remembered and interpreted a dream of a king with implications in the future and with trans-generational significance till date [Daniel 2]).

When you have no purpose for your life, you end up living the purpose of other people and allow purposeless people to waste your time, drain and deplete your resources and sap your energy. Where there is no purpose, there will be a bankruptcy of wisdom. The more purposeful you are, the wiser you act. **<u>Lack of wisdom is</u> revealing your secrets to a prostitute who did not hide her intentions to kill you as Samson did in Judges 16.** That's why people of wisdom don't act recklessly or carelessly. A purposeful life leads to a sound mind.

When you have no plans for your life, you end up living the plans of other people.

Don't ever feel obligated and pressured into another person's plan if it's not in line with yours.

When you have no agenda for your life, you end up living and fulfilling the agenda of other people.

3 REALMS THAT PEOPLE LIVE IN TERMS OF FINANCIAL SUPPLIES:

I.   Poor people live in the realm of not enough

II.   Average people live in the realm of just enough but

III. Covenant-practising people [Genesis 8:22; Luke 6:38; Ephesians 4:28; 2 Corinthians 8; Philippians 4:15-18] live in the realm of far above enough where 5% of your income is too much for all who depend on you to live; before you recover from the last one, another has landed i.e. you live in the realm where you feed nations (Genesis 12:1-3; 13:1-3; 22:16-18; Isaiah 45:1-3; Psalm 45:10-17; 2 Chronicles 25:9). You are not moving from testimony to testimony but rather, you live inside testimony. You live in testimonies and become the testimony [2 Corinthians 9:8; Philippians 4.19; Ephesians 3.20; Job 1:3; John 10:10; 2 Chronicles 25:9; Matthew 5:13-16]

BEFORE YOU NEED IT, IT IS THERE!!!

12. WORK HARD AND WORK SMART:

Success consists of little daily efforts and failure consists of little daily neglects.

Eventually, whatever you are doing right now is producing an INEVITABLE FUTURE.

Success and enlargement or becoming an achiever cannot be inherited; it has to be practically earned through working out deliberate steps.

REMEMBER: It is work that determines worth both in the kingdom and secular world.

You cannot climb the ladder of success with your hands in your pocket.

In the school of success, Joe Girard said: "The elevator to success is (always) out of order. You'll have to use the stairs... one step at a time."

ONE CAN NEVER BE POOR WHILST ONE'S HEAD AND HANDS ARE BEING PUT TO WISE AND SMART WORK.

Hard work is not a curse.

Only Hard Workers Become High Flyers!

Proverbs 22:29, *"Seest thou a man diligent in his business? he shall stand before kings; he shall not stand before mean men."*

Hard work does not weary or tire people out; it's wrong work that does. Hard work within purpose does not weary or tire people out; it's wrong work outside purpose that does.

Hard work within the borders and boundaries of your purpose, gifts, talents and strengths never wearies or tires you out; it's wrong work outside the borders and boundaries of your purpose, gifts, talents and strengths that does.

When you are working hard and smart in your field of calling or endeavour, to you, it's equivalent to being on a vacation. Doing what you both love and like doing within your purpose, calling, vocation, profession, career or assignment, gives you both satisfaction and fulfilment in life. I enjoy preaching teaching, writing, training, praying, singing, worshipping, raising leaders, developing and empowering people, holding seminars and summits. I am wired for this! Besides my love for God, kingdom and my wife 'of course' and family, nothing gives me greater satisfaction than this!!

Poverty is a bad boy!

I am too busy for God to be sick or to die now!!!

13. ARE PEOPLE OF VISION AND EXTREMELY FOCUSSED

They envision and visualize success. Whatever the short or long term goal may be, achievers and highly successful people always visualize their success even before achieving it. They keep reminding themselves what exactly they need to achieve knowing very well that: What you see ahead of you determines what you prioritise, focus on, do and pursue in life.

Proverbs 29:18 says, *"Where there is no vision, my people perish [or live aimlessly and carelessly without restraint or constraint]."*

Hebrews 12:1-2, "Therefore, since we are surrounded by such a great cloud of witnesses, **let us throw off everything that hinders and the sin that so easily entangles. And let us run with perseverance the race marked out for us, fixing our eyes on Jesus, the pioneer and perfecter of faith.** For the joy set before him he endured the cross, scorning its shame, and sat down at the right hand of the throne of God."

What you see ahead of you or your future drives your daily routine.

The Abraham Lincoln story:

A typical example was Abraham Lincoln who despite all the odds that were stacked against him overcame them to become the sixteenth president of the USA.

The power of concentration gives you the mental picture of tomorrow's success as an encouragement, (Hebrews 12:1-2) thus providing you with sustaining power. There are instructions connected to every vision and dream from God. Your discipline and diligence to follow explicitly these instructions will earn you an enviable and a colourful end. **This is what is called The Law of CONCENTRATION.**

You may experience failures or disappointments in the pursuit of your vision or assignment in life but that is not the end.

YOUR PRESENT POSITION IS NOT YOUR PERMANENT ADDRESS!

YOUR PRESENT SITUATION IS NOT YOUR INDEFINITE STATUS!

Abraham Lincoln became the sixteenth president of the United States of America primarily because of **The Law of FOCUS or CONCENTRATION.**

Though he failed many times, he did not give up the pursuit of his destiny.

Listen to his story:

1831 - He failed in business

1832 - He was defeated in running for the legislature

1833 - He failed in business again

1835 - His sweetheart died

1836 - He had a nervous breakdown

1838 - He was defeated in his quest to be speaker of the house

1840 - He was defeated in election

1843 - He was defeated whilst running for congress

1855 - He was defeated whilst running for the senate

1856 - He was defeated whilst running for vice presidency

1858 - He was defeated whilst running for the senate

1860 - He became the sixteenth president of the USA

Great men and women have many stories of disappointments and failures; but they did not allow the negative happenings around them to halt their progress in the pursuit of their dreams. It is your turn to make a difference in the world. Get back your focus. Only one appointment can change your destiny, so forget about the many disappointments. When you finally succeed, the pain of separation, mockery, betrayal, abandonment, loneliness, shame, disgrace, disgrace, rejection, preparation, sacrifice, failures, false accusations, being stigmatised, ostracised and experiencing disappointments will become history to you.

14. THEY LITERALLY DESIGN THEIR SUCCESS AND THEIR FUTURE

Success and enlargement in any laudable venture is not by default but by design.

Success has no uncles; success is self-determined. [*1]

15. DELIBERATELY AND CONSCIOUSLY PLAN EACH DAY WITH PURPOSE AND ACTION.

To the average or normal person, Sunday night gets a bad rep because it means having to face another week, back on the treadmill, spinning the wheel once again but the opposite is true of exceptionally successful people.

On the contrary, achievers and exceptionally Successful people look forward with excitement to the beginning of each week because they are about to do what they love doing which brings them fulfilment so they consciously, deliberately and purposefully plan their days (yes, even Sundays) to be different, better, more exciting, more purposeful, more fruitful, more productive and more meaningful. Tony Robbins says 'action without <u>a higher degree of purpose</u> is a waste of time.'

Success is not by default but by design, so, the question is, how much of your life are you designing or leaving to chance?

Life is not determined by chances but by choices.

Anyone who leaves his life to chance doesn't stand a chance.

"We all have two choices: We can make a living or we can design a life." — Jim Rohn

"No man has a chance to enjoy permanent success until he begins to look in a mirror for the real cause of all his mistakes." - Napoleon Hill

Remember: Success is not by default but by design. Success consists of little daily efforts and failure consists of little daily neglects. Success has no uncles. Success is not by chance but by choice.

16. STEP OUTSIDE THEIR COMFORT ZONE.

Successful people thrive when they are stretched beyond what they think they can handle. They consistently push the boundaries of what's possible and don't accept settling for the status quo. This means <u>stepping outside our comfort zone</u> and questioning the world around us, looking for opportunities to constantly improve. The more we stretch, the greater our capacity. Even Jesus had to be stretched to accomplish His purpose in life as he clearly stated in Luke 12:50, *"But I have a baptism to be baptized with; and how am I straitened (stretched) till it be accomplished!"*

How long have you been in your comfort zone? Become a trail blazer, a path finder, a pace setter and chart a new course. Don't settle for the status quo; break records and set new ones, raise the bar on yourself, set new standards, become outstanding in your field till you become the standard that others must emulate.

17. SURROUND THEMSELVES WITH SMART PEOPLE.
(Refer confidants, constituents and comrades)

Surround yourself or associate with people as pregnant as you or more pregnant than you. (Mary & Elizabeth) Some of the world's trailblazing entrepreneurs, such as Bill Gates, Steve Jobs, Richard Branson and Mark Zuckerberg, had a solid team around them from the beginning—they knew their team was crucial to their success. Collaboration allows you to refine your thinking and challenge yourself and be challenged. We become the average of the five closest people we surround ourselves with.

So, the question is: Who are you spending your time with? Who are you learning from because Success breeds success.

These scriptures are vital in your choices — Psalm 1:1-3; Proverbs 13:20 & 22; Proverbs 27:17, *'As iron sharpens iron, so one person sharpens another.'*

Charles "Tremendous" Jones said: *"You are the same person today that you will be in five years except for two things; The books you read and the people you associate with."*

Take these tips as capsules to improve your life and fulfil your destiny.

Challenge yourself on a daily basis.

Never give up.

Surround yourself with great people who will encourage you to move forward, to read more, know more, do more, achieve more and fulfil destiny.

Bishop T. D. Jakes taught on 3 Basic People You Will Meet and Interact with in life i.e. **Confidants, Constituents and Comrades** i.e. - A A plus; A- B; B plus B-; C Plus C-

He said: "To be covered by God and to walk in the area of your destiny, you can't afford to be limited by walking with people who look like you all the time". There are 3 basic types and kinds of people that you will interact with if you are a child of destiny.

The 1ˢᵗ Group are Confidants:

You will have very few of them.

Confidants are those people in your life who love you unconditionally; they are into you whether you are, up or down, right or wrong they are into you; they are in for the long haul. If you get in trouble, they will get in the trouble with you; they will come to see you in the jail house, they will come and get you out of the crack house. They are confidants whom you can open up and share anything with them. You will never inherit your kingdom until you find your confidant. You can't be David until you find your Jonathan. As a David, you need a Jonathan as your confidant. Having a good confidant is the key that unlocks the kingdom because you were raised outside the gate and God is gonna cause you to reach over the wall; you've got to have a confidant behind the wall who can mentor you to do what God is going to do next in your life, You need a mentor who will help you...

The problem with most people is that everybody they run around with is under them and so you are forever feeding people who can't feed you; you always walking and associating with people who you are always feeding who can't feed you and who can't empower you and after years of feeding and empowering them, they begin to drain you, criticise you and desert you. You've got to have somebody who can feed you so you can feed somebody else. You need a confidant then. A confidant is the few unavoidable people that come along in your life that are for you, they are with you, they are intimately intertwined in your life, they are there to make sure you reach your destiny not desert you a quarter, halfway or three-quarter way. They will confront you, challenge you, encourage you to be better; they will be in your face, they will get in your business and they will tell you when you are wrong because they are confidants. If you have two or three of them in a lifetime, you are a blessed person; without them, you will not be who God called you to be, SO YOU NEED TO FIND YOUR CONFIDANT.

The 2nd Group are your Constituents:

They are not into you but they are into what you are for; they are for what you are for i.e. they are your constituents. They are for what you are for and as long as you are for what you are for, they will walk with you and work with you and labour with you but never think that they are for you; they are for what you are for and you have to know that because if and when they meet someone else who will further their agenda, they will leave you and hook up with them because they were never for you but were just for what you were for. They are your constituents and throughout your life if you are not careful particularly if you are broken, you will mistake your constituents for your confidants with very serious, disastrous, detrimental consequences causing irreparable damage which can scar you for life. By their actions you can mistake your constituents for your confidants by thinking or assuming that they are for you when they are really not for you; they are just for what you are for and by the time you get through falling in love with them, they will break your heart as they hook up with somebody else who is for what you are for because it was never about you anyway. It was about the causes that you represent; they are for what you are for but they are not for you because they are just your constituents.

The 3ʳᵈ Group are your Comrades:

These people are not for you nor are they for what you are for. It is just that they are against what you are against. These comrades will make strange bedfellows which will cause or make people who are not for you to come together yet are not for what you are for but are against what you are against and they will team up with you to help fight a greater enemy but don't be confused by their associations with you because they will only be with you until the victory is accomplished. These people are like scaffolding; they come into your life to fulfil a purpose and when the purpose is complete, the scaffolding is removed but don't be upset when they or the scaffolding is removed because the building always remains standing when the scaffolding is removed. What am saying to you is: expect the constituents and the comrades to leave you and desert you after a while. Don't be upset when they don't react to your dream the way you expected them to when you expected them to because they were never really with you in the first place.

[1 John 2:19 NIV says, *"They went out from us, but they did not really belong to us. For if they had belonged to us, they would have remained with us; but their going showed that none of them belonged to us."*]

Be careful then who you tell your dream to because if you tell your dream to your constituents, they will desert you and try to fulfil the dream without you. If you tell your dream to your comrades, they won't support it because they were never for what you were for anyway. If you find a few people in your entire life with whom you can share your dreams with, you are a blessed somebody.

I can tell you how to identify those who are really for you no matter what!

If they are really for you, they will weep with you when you weep, rejoice with you when you rejoice, be with you both when you are up and when you are down, in your successes and in your failure, in your strong moments and in your weak moments when you don't have and when you have, when you are a nobody and when you become somebody. They are not deserters of ship when the boat starts rocking or when you or they are going through personal challenges; they don't forget easily what you've done for them, don't abandon you, betray you, accuse you or leave you or deny you what's due you, no matter what. They are not for sale at any price or to the highest bidder. Whenever you walk into a room and tell them your good news, stop for a minute and watch their reaction; if they are not happy for you, shut your mouth and walk out of the door because when they are really connected to you, they will be happy for you when you share your dream. Ask your neighbour, Are you happy for me? If your success clearly makes someone unhappy, that's a clear sign to you; you don't need a prophet or an angel to advise you to flee. If Someone feels their failure is because of your success, you must disassociate immediately. God is so faithful He will always send you a helper. If God ever sent you some people to help you, rejoice; don't worry about the people he took. Praise him for the people he sent!"

"Success is going from failure to failure without loss of enthusiasm."
– Winston Churchill

Ecclesiastes 3:1, "To every thing there is a season, and a time to every purpose under the heaven:"

18. FOCUS ON THE BIG PICTURE.

Focusing on details allows you to <u>track results</u> and make improvements based on facts, not guesswork. But sometimes, we get lost in the *doing* and forget the *building* and *creating*. If you are not designing and creating a better life for yourself, who will? Never lose sight of the big picture and always work on your why. You are either designing a life or cruising through life. The Billionaire mindset says, 'Either you design your life or somebody else will do it for you.' Just as: No one's success is the reason for your failure in life, neither is anyone's failure, the reason for your success in life. Surprisingly: The truth is: Success is self-determined!

19. GET THE JOB THEY'VE SET THEIR HEARTS AND HANDS ON DONE.

Proverbs 22:29, *"Seest thou a man diligent in his business? he shall stand before kings; he shall not stand before mean men."*

Proverbs 12:24, New Living Translation, *"Work hard and become a leader; Be lazy and become a slave."*

NIV *"Diligent hands will rule, but laziness ends in forced labor."*

It's human behaviour to procrastinate but High achievers have developed laser-like focus when it comes to getting things done. Most times they can be so obsessed with their assignment in life that others call them selfish and unsociable often making sacrifices most of us are not prepared or willing to make.

WHAT DIFFERENTIATES EXTRAORDINARY PEOPLE FROM ORDINARY PEOPLE?

Extraordinary people are simply ordinary people who went the extra mile to do something extra that other ordinary people were not willing to do and outstanding people are simply people who chose not to remain average or settle for mediocrity or the status quo but to stand out of the crowd or among many and to prioritise priorities.

<u>Prioritize better</u>; set aside time to focus on your goals list, not your to-do list. If you sleep 8 hours a day you've slept a third of your life i.e. 30 out of 90 years or 40 out of 120 years.

20. ARE HIGHLY MOTIVATED

They are ALWAYS positive.

Achievers and Highly successful people deliberately and consciously spend most of their time with positive-minded people and resource materials. They don't have time to waste with people who always focus on negative things. Not only that, high achievers and successful people focus on positive aspects when undergoing rough patches in life.

21. DREAM ONLY BIG DREAMS

Joseph dreamed and dreamed yet another dream seeing his brethren bow before him in Genesis 37.

David said, 'Is there not a cause?'; I can take on Goliath in 1 Samuel 17.

"The biggest adventure you can ever take is to live the life of your dreams." – Oprah Winfrey

"It may be that those who do most, dream most." – Stephen Leacock

"The future belongs to those who believe in the beauty of their dreams." – Eleanor Roosevelt

"There is only one thing that makes a dream impossible to achieve: the fear of failure." – Paulo Coelho.

"Dreams are the touchstones of our characters." – Henry David Thoreau.

22. THEY CAN ALWAYS SEE THE FUTURE THEY DESIRE TO ARRIVE AT

You cannot arrive at a future you cannot see!

Genesis 13:15, *"**All** the land that you see I will give to you and your offspring forever."*

If you can't see it in your spirit, you can't be it or reach it.

"If you can dream it, you can do it. Always remember that this whole thing was started with a dream and a mouse." – Walt Disney

"I don't dream at night, I dream all day; I dream for a living." – Steven Spielberg

"The biggest adventure you can ever take is to live the life of your dreams." – Oprah Winfrey

23. USE THEIR MINDS PRODUCTIVELY

'It is when your mind is put to work that the natural resources becomes meaningful and relevant.' - Bishop David Abioye

24. THEY USE THEIR HEAD BY BEING CREATIVE AND INNOVATIVE

It is only those who use their head who stay ahead in life!

25. THEY ARE VERY MINDFUL OF THE 3 A's

THE 3 A's that determine how you are perceived and received in the high echelons of society.

I.   Appearance

II.   Attitude

III.   Achievements

The first introduction we have of God is as an achiever – GOD CREATED as stated in Genesis 1:1-2, *"In the beginning God created the heavens and the earth. Now the earth was formless and empty, darkness was over the surface of the deep, and the Spirit of God was hovering over the waters."*

26. ARE ARDENT READERS

You cannot be an effective leader without being an ardent reader, you cannot be an ardent reader without being a creative thinker, you cannot be a creative thinker without generating ideas, you cannot generate ideas without being a hard and smart worker and you cannot be a smart and hard worker without becoming fabulously affluential (rich and influential.)

1 Timothy 4:13-15, *"Till I come, give attendance to reading, to exhortation, to doctrine. Neglect not the gift that is in thee, which was given thee by prophecy, with the laying on of the hands of the presbytery. Meditate upon these things; give thyself wholly to them; that thy profiting may appear to all."*

Henry Ford said: 'Anyone who stops learning is old, whether at twenty or eighty. Anyone who keeps learning stays young whether at twenty or eighty. The greatest thing in life therefore, is to keep your mind young.'

27. ARE RISK-TAKERS i.e. They Take Risks; THEY ARE STEP-TAKERS AND MOVE-MAKERS

2 Kings 7:3-4, NIV, *"Now there were four men with leprosy at the entrance of the city gate. They said to each other, "Why stay here*

until we die? If we say, 'We'll go into the city'—the famine is there, and we will die. And if we stay here, we will die. So let's go over to the camp of the Arameans and surrender. If they spare us, we live; if they kill us, then we die."

Numbers 13:30, *"Then Caleb silenced the people before Moses and said, "We should go up and take possession of the land, for we can certainly do it."*

Esther 4:16, *"Go, gather together all the Jews that are present in Shushan, and fast ye for me, and neither eat nor drink three days, night or day: I also and my maidens will fast likewise; and so will I go in unto the king, which is not according to the law: and if I perish, I perish."*

If you want to be great, you have got to risk failure. Launch out of your comfort zone.

Is Faith A Risk?

Hebrews 11:8, *"By faith Abraham, when he was called to go out into a place which he should after receive for an inheritance, obeyed; and he went out, (Moved) not knowing whither he went."*

Ask Abraham and the list of heroes in the hall of faith. Following a man of God who does not know where he is going but keeps saying he is following God (Genesis 12, 13, 14, 18) is a risk. Faith is not a risk; faith is the victory that overcomes the world.

1 John 5:4, NIV, *"for everyone born of God overcomes the world. This is the victory that has overcome the world, even our faith."*

1 John 5:4, ESV, *"For everyone who has been born of God overcomes the world."*

Obeying God and walking by faith is a risk but a risk worth taking because we have the assurance of the word that is forever settled and ever reliable. (Romans 4:17-21; Ps. 119:89)

Also, the whole of God's power, arsenals and integrity is behind His word, (Hebrews 4:12; Jeremiah 1:12; Hebrews 1:3) because He upholds all things by the word of His power.

Every man or woman of Faith is a step-taker and move-maker. Noah moved by faith and Abraham moved by faith. Whatever does not make you move will not create any waves. It is Move-Makers that are Wave-Makers!! Bible and Authentic Faith comes with energy to act or take steps. People of faith take steps and make moves. It is not possible to be in faith and be stationary, at a standstill or stagnant.

Faith does not make you sit down and be wishing or waiting for things; rather, faith moves you and makes you go after things and to make things happen because faith without works or steps is dead. Therefore, Step out and make things happen for your total health and total prosperity because God enlarges your steps i.e. the steps you take.

Psalm 18:36, *"Thou hast enlarged my steps under me, that my feet did not slip."* Like he did with the lepers both in 2 Kings 7 and in Luke 17:14, *"When he saw them, he said, "Go, show yourselves to the priests."*

AND AS THEY WENT, THEY WERE CLEANSED or HEALED. Not As they SAT!

Mark 2:5 says, *"When he saw their faith..."*

SO, FAITH CAN BE SEEN!

From Hebrews 11, we discover that all the heroes in the hall of faith were doers, movers, step-takers. That's why A.A. Allen said: "When you run out of faith, (action) you run out of the supernatural."

The move of man provokes the move of God; you act correctly and God reacts massively. The lepers asked, 'Why sit we here till we die?' (2 Kings 7:3-6)

You are not a candidate of pity but of envy. (Genesis 26:12-14)

What Is Risk?

Stepping out of your comfort zone to achieve something new or a feat

- a situation involving exposure to danger to achieve a goal

- Investing in something new to make profit

- **Finding new paths, taking new steps, setting new paces, new standards, charting new courses, breaking and setting new records and blazing new trails i.e. Becoming a pathfinder, pace setter, course charter, record breaker, new record and standard setter and trail blazer.**

"Do not follow where the path may lead. Go instead where there is no path and leave a trail." – Ralph Waldo Emerson

You never know what you can achieve or do until you step out of your comfort zone.

Until you leave your present shores, you can never discover new lands or take new territories.

If you don't climb the mountain, you can't view the plain and IF YOU DON'T LIVE ON THE EDGE, YOU WILL NEVER SEE THE VIEW.

Until you live on the edge, you will never see the view.

Take risks: if you win you will be happy; if you lose you will be wiser.

Why do many people refuse to take Risks in their life?

FEAR: Fear of failure, change, people's opinion, what people will think of them, criticism, mockery, imaginary lions in the streets, fear of tomorrow, price you must pay, hard work, giving, sacrifices, shame or disgrace or losing money or everything if it doesn't work, fear of growing old, etc.

As Lewis Carroll said: In the end we only regret the chances we did not take!!

Story of Colonel Sanders, founder of KFC

"At age 5 his Father died," <u>begins the story</u>. "At age 16 he quit school. At age 17 he had already lost four jobs. At age 18 he got married. He joined the army and washed out there. At age 20 his wife left him and took their baby. He became a cook in a small cafe and convinced his wife to return home. At age 65 he retired. He felt like a failure and decided to commit suicide. He sat writing his will, but instead, he wrote what he would have accomplished with his life & thought about how good of a cook he was. So he borrowed $87 fried up some chicken using his recipe, went door to door to sell. At age 88 Colonel Sanders, founder of Kentucky Fried Chicken (KFC) Empire was a billionaire."

What are the consequences of avoiding Risks in life?

Non-achievement, not making history, not changing levels or status in life, staying in one spot, living a life of regrets, staying ordinary, stagnation, doubting, wandering and asking yourself continuously 'what if?' Not knowing what could have been possible. (Contrary to the bold steps of Caleb and Joshua in Numbers 13:30 and David in 1 Samuel 17)

Like David, rise up and despite ridicule, boldly declare 'Is there not a cause?' and go forward, face your Goliath and become all you were born and created to be and to do.

You will be surprised to know that: What separates the rich from the poor is what also separates risk-takers from non risk-takers!

It's the same reason the rich are getting richer and the poor are getting poorer.

Mike Murdock said: Your hatred of the rich may explain your poverty i.e. why you are poor.

I said: Your hatred of achievers and risk takers may explain your non-achievement and inability to take risks.

Certain people's hatred of the rich may explain their poverty and certain people's hatred of achievers may explain their non-achievement and stagnation in life!!

Distinguishing Factors Between Risk-Takers And Non Risk-Takers:

I. Mentality:

Right mentality vs. wrong mentality

Cruise mentality vs. purpose-driven mentality

Entitlement mentality vs. taking full responsibility mentality

Working mentality vs. waiting or wishing mentality

Hard and smart work Mentality vs. lazy mentality

*** **Mentality matters in this journey of life.**

II. Attitude to life:

Attitude has everything to do with success, progress, acceleration, achievement, accomplishment and fulfilment in life.

Attitude determines altitude in life.

A stinking attitude leads to a stinking life; a rude attitude leads to a rude awakening at a certain age in life, but a good attitude brings you into all the goodies and privileges in life.

Your attitude to time i.e. timeliness, punctuality, being early, on time or late all the time

III. Choices in life:

Life is about choices.

Choices determine decisions.

Right choices lead to good decisions and wrong choices lead to bad decisions.

Every road has a destination. He who chooses the beginning of a road also chooses its outcome and destination.

That's why Moses said to the Israelites in Deuteronomy 30:19 (NIV), "This day I call the heavens and the earth as witnesses against you that I have set before you life and death, blessings and curses. **Now choose life, so that you and your children may live."**

Joshua 24:15 (NIV), *"But if serving the* LORD *seems undesirable to you,* ***then choose for yourselves this day whom you will serve,*** *whether the gods your ancestors served beyond the Euphrates, or the gods of the Amorites, in whose land you are living.* ***But as for me and my household, we will [CHOOSE TO] serve the*** LORD***."***

THE KEY WORD IS: CHOOSE! LIFE IS ABOUT CHOICES!!

Achievers, Risk-takers, the successful and the rich make themselves rich by what they CHOOSE TO DO OR CHOOSE NOT TO DO! They become achievers by what they do and don't do; surprisingly the poor also make themselves poor by what they do and don't do which they must do.

Proverbs 22:13, *"The slothful man saith, There is a lion without, I shall be slain in the streets."*

He made a choice so ended up poor.

IV. Approach and attitude to hard work and smart work i.e. DILIGENCE:

Proverbs 10:4, NIV, *"Lazy hands make for poverty, but diligent hands bring wealth."*

Proverbs 22:29, *"Seest thou a man diligent in his business? he shall stand before kings; he shall not stand before mean men."*

Proverbs 12:24, New Living Translation, *"Work hard and become a leader; Be lazy and become a slave."*

"The hand of the diligent shall bear rule; but the slothful shall be under tribute."

We are either Finding reasons for our success or giving excuses for our failures!

"As a door turns on its hinges, so a sluggard turns on his bed. A sluggard buries his hand in the dish; he is too lazy to bring it back to his mouth. A sluggard is wiser in his own eyes than seven people who answer discreetly." (Proverbs 26:14-16 NIV)

RISK-TAKERS HAVE THIS PHILOSOHY: Work for others, work for yourself and then work for posterity. They think, see, prepare and plan for the future. They live today with the future clearly in mind not just today.

V. Vision or lack of vision:

What you see ahead of you determines what you prioritise, focus on, do and pursue in life. (Proverbs 29:18)
What you see drives your daily routine. Success consists of little daily efforts and failure consists of little daily neglects.

VI. Time Management:

In life you are either marking time, wasting time or investing time.

Every time wasted on frivolities is destiny-wasted. Life is like a timetable; wisdom is the ability to do the right thing at the right time to generate the right results.

Ecclesiastes 3:1, *"There is a time for everything and a season for every activity under heaven."*

Ecclesiastes 11:1, *"Cast your bread upon the waters and you shall find it after many days."*

THREE KINDS OF PEOPLE:

a. Those who do yesterday's things today i.e. BEHIND TIME. Therefore are late in life and having to catch up. It's sad to see People who are late in life but have no sense of urgency.

b. Those who do today's things today i.e. ON TIME.

c. Those who do tomorrow's things today i.e. AHEAD OF TIME. (a typical example was Joseph who received wisdom to solve a 14 years problem ahead of time [Genesis 41]; Daniel remembering and interpreting a dream with implications in the future and with trans-generational significance till date [Daniel 2]).

VII. Habits:

Wrong or right and destructive or constructive habits.

"Men's natures are alike; it is their habits that separate them." – **Confucius**

"We are what we repeatedly do. Excellence then, is not an act, but a habit." – **Aristotle**

Risk-takers adopt good habits they live by daily.

VIII. Wisdom or lack of it:

Wisdom is knowing the right thing to do and doing it, knowing the right step to take and taking it and knowing the right way to go and going there or heading in that direction.

Why? Wisdom is profitable to direct. (Ecclesiastes 10:10)

IX. Associations:

Associations are crucial to success in life in general. You increase in life by association, you decrease in life by association and you also stay stagnant in life by association.

Psalm 1:1-3, "Blessed is the man that walketh not in the counsel of the ungodly, nor standeth in the way of sinners, nor sitteth in the seat of the scornful. But his delight is in the law of the Lord; and in his law doth he meditate day and night. And he shall be like a tree planted by the rivers of water, that bringeth forth his fruit in his season; his leaf also shall not wither; and whatsoever he doeth shall prosper."

WHEN PURPOSE IS DISCOVERED, RELATIONSHIPS ARE TRIMMED!

X. Personal development or lack of it:

If all you know is all you learnt or knew from school in this competitive world where you must have competitive advantage, you are way behind schedule and off target. WHAT YOU KNEW YESTERDAY IS NOT ENOUGH TO TAKE YOU TO YOUR NEXT LEVEL.

Abraham Lincoln said, "I don't care much about anyone who is not wiser today than they were yesterday."

There are three types of people in life and where they are is all by choice; they made themselves this way. Those who are behind schedule, those who are on schedule and those who are ahead of schedule.

XI. Planning For Posterity or Just Today:

Risk-takers, achievers, the rich, wealthy, influential and the successful always live today with tomorrow in mind. If you aren't there yet, you must come to a place on your own in your life where you start thinking of, preparing for and planning for the future i.e. Succession, Posterity i.e. generations yet unborn.

Every day you must be planning and building for the future By Investing In, Adding Value to yourself and others and raising others with what you know. You must develop and maintain A Posterity and Succession Mentality and Attitude throughout.

Why? Success without a successor is failure. Your greatest legacy is your spiritual legacy i.e. pouring into souls i.e. people. Leaving or duplicating yourself in others. (Matthew 28:18-20; Daniel 12:3)

***Stardom Comes With Winning the souls of men

"Those who are wise will shine like the brightness of the heavens, and those who lead many to righteousness, like the stars for ever and ever." - Daniel 12:3 NIV

God Pays Soul Winners and Those Who Prioritise His Kingdom Interests "And he that reapeth receiveth wages, and gathereth fruit unto life eternal: that both he that soweth and he that reapeth may rejoice together." - John 4:36; Matthew 6:33

XII. A life of generosity or stinginess:

"There is that scattereth, and yet increaseth; and there is that withholdeth more than is meet, but it tendeth to poverty." - Proverbs 11:24

Life is not measured in duration but in donations.

XIII. Prompt Obedience or Procrastinating:

> Example of Abraham's prompt obedience in Genesis 12, 14, 18, 22

28. THEY KEEP THEIR MINDS YOUNG

THE ANSWER FOR OLD AGE: Keep Your Mind Young And Never say 'I am aged or old.'

Henry Ford said: 'Anyone who stops learning is old, whether at twenty or eighty. Anyone who keeps learning stays young whether at twenty or eighty. The greatest thing in life therefore, is to keep your mind young.'

There are three ages, chronological, biological, and psychological.

The first is calculation based on our date of birth; the second is determined by the health conditions; the third is how old we feel. While we don't have control over the first, we can take care of our health with good diet, exercise and have or maintain a cheerful attitude.

Proverbs 17:22, *"A merry heart doeth good like a medicine: but a broken spirit drieth the bones."*

A positive attitude and optimistic thinking can reverse the third age.

Proverbs 23:7, *"As a man thinketh in his heart, so he is."*

Denis Waitley said: "If you think you can, you can."

The opposite is also true: IF YOU THINK YOU CAN'T, YOU CAN'T!

Henry Ford SAID: Whether you think you can, or you think you can't, you're right.

29. THEY LIVE PREPARED AND IN READINESS MODE DAILY:

They are ever Learning To Answer Tomorrow's Questions Today:

When preparation meets opportunity, success is inevitable. Success occurs when preparation meets opportunity.

Preparedness refers to a very concrete research based set of actions that are taken as precautionary measures in the face of potential disasters. These actions can include both physical preparations (such as emergency supplies depots, adapting buildings to survive earthquakes and so on) and trainings for emergency action. Preparedness is an important quality in achieving goals and in avoiding and mitigating negative outcomes. There are different types of preparedness, such as public health preparedness and local <u>emergency preparedness</u> or snow preparedness (i.e.: Snow Preparedness Teams - SPT), but probably the most developed type is "Disaster Preparedness", defined by the UN as involving "forecasting and taking precautionary measures prior to an imminent threat when advance warnings are possible".[1] This includes not only natural disasters, but all kinds of severe damage caused in a relatively short period, including warfare. Preparedness is a major phase of <u>emergency management</u>, and is particularly valued in areas of <u>competition</u> such as <u>sport</u> and <u>military science</u>.

Methods of preparation include <u>research</u>, <u>estimation</u>, <u>planning</u>, resourcing, <u>education</u>, practicing and <u>rehearsing</u>.

30. DEMAND MORE FROM THEMSELVES:

"Be willing to be uncomfortable. Be comfortable being uncomfortable. It may get tough, but it's a small price to pay for living a dream." – Peter McWilliams.

2 Timothy 3:14-17, *"But continue thou in the things which thou hast learned and hast been assured of, knowing of whom thou hast learned them; And that from a child thou hast known the holy scriptures, which are able to make thee wise unto salvation through faith which is in Christ Jesus. All scripture is given by inspiration of God, and is profitable for doctrine, for reproof, for correction, for instruction in righteousness: That the man of God may be perfect, thoroughly furnished unto all good works."*

"If you are facing a new challenge or being asked to do something that you have never done before don't be afraid to step out. You have more capacity than you think you do but you will never see it unless you place a demand on yourself for more." – Joyce Meyer.

A life of average and mediocrity may do us no harm at the moment, but down the line it will lead to dissatisfaction and regrets. God doesn't want us to be ordinary; we have everything it takes to do far greater than we can ever imagine. God is *"… able, through His mighty power at work within us, to accomplish infinitely more than we might ask or think"* - Ephesians 3:20

2 Chronicles 25:9 tells us HE CAN GIVE US FAR MORE THAN THIS.

To get the best out of everything we do, we need to ask more from ourselves than anyone will ever ask.

"Ninety-nine percent of the failures come from people who have the habit of making excuses" - George Washington Carver.

Too often we wish or wait for a miracle when we should be working out a miracle. One of the gifts of the Spirit is the gift of working of miracles not the gift of waiting or wishing for miracles.

1 Corinthians 12:10, *"To another the working of miracles; to another prophecy; to another discerning of spirits; to another divers kinds of tongues; to another the interpretation of tongues:"*

So, it is worked at not waited or wished for.

God says, *"Whatever you do, work at it with all your heart…"* (Colossians 3:2).

Steve Maraboli said, "The universe doesn't give you what you want in your mind, it gives you what you demand with your actions".

Fortunately, we all know what we need to change, but unfortunately there seems to always be something within and outside us that always seems to stand in the way.

To succeed, we need to demand more from ourselves. We need to challenge ourselves to explore new territories. Talent doesn't really do much. As important as talent may be, hard work is the hallmark of all winners. Stretching ourselves will move us beyond boundaries. As the saying goes, 'Until you leave your present shores you never discover new lands or new territories.'

The more we stretch, the greater our capacity. Even Jesus had to be stretched to accomplish his purpose in life as he clearly stated in Luke 12:50, *"But I have a baptism to be baptized with; and how am I straitened (stretched) till it be accomplished!"*

The only snag is, stretching often hurts, and not everyone enjoys that experience. But the truth is 'Anyone that refuses to grow or develop themselves will remain in the past.' It is a demand of life.

Nothing beats hard work or diligence. Proverbs 12:24, ESV, 'The hand of the diligent will rule, while the slothful will be put to forced labor."

Proverbs 14:23 ESV *"In all toil there is profit, but mere talk tends only to poverty."*

Proverbs 22:29 ESV, *"Do you see a man skillful in his work? He will stand before kings; he will not stand before obscure men."*

"Seest thou a man diligent in his business? he shall stand before kings; he shall not stand before mean men."

Proverbs 127:1-2, *"Except the Lord build the house, they labour in vain that build it: except the Lord keep the city, the watchman waketh but in vain. It is vain for you to rise up early, to sit up late, to eat the bread of sorrows: for so he giveth his beloved sleep."*

"When you demand higher standards for yourself, you are preparing for the next level" – Unknown source

John 9:4, *"I must work the works of him that sent me, while it is day: the night cometh, when no man can work."*

John 4:34, *"Jesus saith unto them, My meat is to do the will of him that sent me, and to finish his work."*

31. THEY GIVE EVERY ENDEAVOUR THE BEST THEY CAN AND BECOME THE BEST THEY CAN.

THEY PUT IN MAXIMIUM EFFORT KNOWING VERY WELL THAT MAXIMUM EFFORT LEADS TO MAXIMUM ACHIEVEMENT.

"The thoughts of the diligent tend only to plenteousness; but of every one that is hasty only to want." (Proverbs 21:5)

Productivity means product of activity!

Satan is after and rejoices over the failure of God's people.

Helen Hayes states the difference between achievement and success as narrated by her mother: "Achievement is the knowledge that you have studied and worked hard and done the best that is in you. Success is being praised by others, and that's nice too, but not as important or satisfying. Always aim for achievement and forget about success." Bits & Pieces, August, 1989.

God wants us to maximise our potential.

Under-achievement is characterised by fear of commitment to success-related activities, lack of belief in one's self and avoidance of tasks that are challenging. We can achieve to any extent we aim at, *"…with man this is impossible, but with God all things are possible."* (Matthew 19:26).

Achievers embrace challenges and take chances. In life competition is important, but satisfaction is more important. The feeling that you have done your best is more important than anything else. Our job is to keep doing our best, but it has to really be the best.

We can achieve a lot more. Commit yourself to maximising your potential, take the first step, continue taking small steps daily, be prepared to go through the temporal pains that lead to success and God will see you through in Jesus name.

Under-achievers believe that success is based on luck and so, leave things to drift and take no personal responsibility for their progress. Many people believe they lack the ability and resources to reach their next level of success, and prefer to remain within their comfort zone. We need to keep pressing *"...toward the mark for the prize of the high calling of God in Christ Jesus"* (Philippians 3:14).

SUCCESS CONSISTS OF LITTLE DAILY EFFORTS; FAILURE CONSISTS OF LITTLE DAILY NEGLECTS!

It is not reasonable to expect maximum results with minimum effort. We are the only ones that can tell whether we are putting our best into achieving our goals.

"Don't settle for average. Bring your best to the moment. Then, whether it fails or succeeds, at least you know you gave all you had. We need to give the best that is in us." (Angela Bassett).

In the long run average actions will yield average results. If we give a dream everything we have, we will get from it everything there is.

"When a man is no longer anxious to do better than well, he is done for." — Benjamin Haydon

Proverbs 24:27, *"Prepare thy work without, and make it fit for thyself in the field; and afterwards build thine house."*

2 Chronicles 15:7, *"Be ye strong therefore, and let not your hands be weak: for your work shall be rewarded."*

32. THEY BELIEVE IN THEMSELVES:

THEY BELIEVE IN WHAT GOD HAS MADE THEM CAPABLE OF ACHIEVING AND WHAT THEY HAVE MADE THEMSELVES CAPABLE OF ACHIEVING AND ACCOMPLISHING.

SELF-BELIEVERS ARE GREAT ACHIEVERS!

"But blessed is the one who trusts in the LORD, whose confidence is in Him" (Jeremiah 17:7).

Apart from believing in God, self-belief is the highest form of belief. In this world we cannot live on our own, a single tree cannot make a forest. We need others in almost everything we do, and without them we will not enjoy true and lasting success. However, we cannot wait until people approve of us before we pursue our dreams.

There will be haters and doubters, who hate to see others succeed. Some will even do everything they can to rob us of our dream. These could be our loved ones or people whose responsibility it is to cheer us into victory. The Bible says, the Lord who *"...began a good work in you will carry it on to completion until the day of Christ Jesus"* (Philippians 1:6).

If we have to wait for people's stamp of approval, we may have to wait forever.

Sometimes, self-belief can be difficult especially when the odds are stack against you, when the facts on ground signal that your chances of success are slim. When things seem to be falling apart, it feels like you are on your own and there is a trail of failure and disappointments behind you, never stop believing in yourself. Celebrate yourself. Compliment yourself. Encourage yourself like David did in 1 Samuel 30:6.

God's Word says, *"…the Lord will be at your side and will keep your foot from being snared"* (Proverbs 3:26). Travel alone, when you need to; if you can carry others along, fine, if not, keep away from doubters and non-believers and pursue your dream with conviction, passion and determination. It is all about you; with or without people's validation you will reach your destination. At some point, they will start to believe in you and even follow you. Most of the famous people in the world today were once rejected; rejected by individuals, family, peers, groups and nations.

Self-believers are great achievers.

"Cast not away therefore your confidence, which hath great recompence of reward." — Hebrews 10:35

"Let us therefore come boldly unto the throne of grace, that we may obtain mercy, and find grace to help in time of need." — Hebrews 4:16

"Some trust in chariots, and some in horses: but we will remember the name of the Lord our God." - Psalms 20:7

"To be a champ, you have to believe in yourself when nobody believes in you" – Sugar Ray Robinson

33. THEY ARE HIGHLY DISCIPLINED AND HAVE AND MAINTAIN VERY WEIRD ROUTINES AND SCHEDULES.

They are highly disciplined and have and maintain weird routines and schedules whilst others are casual and careless about their routines and schedules:

THEY ARE VERY REGIMENTED AND LITERALLY PUT THEIR LIVES ON SCHEDULES. Some of us may have read about the weird sleep and work routines of high achievers and highly successful people. While some successful people develop innovative ideas when asleep, some derive ideas by refusing to sleep!

IMPORTANT SECRETS TO NOTE ABOUT ACHIEVERS:

Very few of us might know that Thomas Edison slept for hardly three hours per day!

Did you know that Beethoven developed ideas in his bathroom? Some people prefer being completely solitary during work time even though some see it as unsociable.

34. THEY ACCEPT CRITICISM AND FEEDBACK

They accept criticism. Achievers and Successful people are open minded so as to accept honest feedback as well as criticism from people. They view it positively and focus on improving themselves.

35. THEY ARE ALWAYS READY FOR NEW IDEAS.

They have the habit of keeping a pen, writing pad or notepad or notes on their phones handy very much aware that ideas come in the form of flashes.

The smallest pen is bigger and better than the biggest brain.

36. THEY DEFINE AND ARE CLEAR ABOUT THEIR RELATIONSHIPS WITH PEOPLE.

Never assume relationships i.e. never ever assume you are in a relationship with anyone. Get your facts right and define clearly your relationships with people before you get your heart irreparably broken.

They walk among and learn from giants so become giants as well.

37. WHEN PEOPLE BETRAY, ABANDON OR LEAVE THEM SUDDENLY, THEY LET THEM GO. THEY DON'T STEW IN THEIR NEGATIVE PAST.

Life has taught me that you can't buy or control someone's loyalty. No matter how good you are to them, doesn't mean they'll treat you the same. No matter how much they mean to you, doesn't mean they'll value you the same. Sometimes the people you love the most, turn out to be the people you can trust the least. - Trent Shelton

No matter what you do or don't do, what you change or don't change, die or live, some people you were close to in the past have made it categorically clear by their actions that they just don't want you back in their lives. Accept it and get on with your life!!!

So, when people walk away from you, let them go. Your destiny is never tied to anyone who leaves you and it does not mean they are bad people either. It just means that their part in your story is over.

REMEMBER: You can't fight a landlord when you are a tenant; it's the highest form of insanity to fight a landlord when you are still a tenant in his house.

"The definition of insanity is doing the same thing over and over again, but **expecting different results**". - Albert Einstein

38. THEY ARE HUMBLE AND PHILANTHROPIC

Being humble and down-to-earth is by far a very peculiar sign of high achievers and highly successful people. They never boast about their achievements and continue life in the routine way.

Listen to this funny statement: RICH PEOPLE STAY RICH BY LIVING LIKE THEY ARE BROKE. BROKE PEOPLE STAY BROKE BY LIVING LIKE THEY'RE RICH!

Also, successful people are engaged in philanthropic activities, to improve lives of several needy people. They believe they have gained a lot from the society. On achieving success, they feel good sharing it back with the society.

39. THEY STAY ORIGINAL AND FOLLOW THEIR HEART

They remain true to their original self without worrying about others' opinions. They never try to be what 'others' want them to be and always follow their heart.

Not only that, they do laugh at themselves; fail many times; never hesitate to ask help from others when needed; accept their shortcomings; dream big!

They stretch themselves beyond their comfort zone.

40. ADDITIONAL Useful tips to become successful: [6]

Sometimes, it is just about overcoming your fears and taking risks in life. If you avoid taking risk, you may not discover your capabilities. Never be afraid of failure, it's very important in finding success.

Fail with an attitude. Fail Forward by learning from past failures. Remember: You are not a failure until you quit. Winners don't quit and quitters don't win.

Follow a healthy routine, exercise regularly, eat well, laugh a lot, sleep peacefully, stop worrying. Have and maintain a sense of humour.

Always maintain your joy. Proverbs 17:22, *"A merry heart doeth good like a medicine: but a broken spirit drieth the bones."*

Sometimes, one needs to stop worrying about things beyond one's control. Instead of dwelling on problems with your mind (worry) use it to create answers (think).

Look for and find opportunities where others give up.

Take complete responsibility for your actions and outcomes or lack of them.

Try being proactive instead of being reactive.

Be sure about yourself and your deeds.

Your looks, your dress does not determine your worth.

**Stop focusing on the shape of your head and focus on what's in your brain.

Learn to swim against the tide.

Have guts to follow only your heart and not the crowd!

Do not take life seriously, learn to have fun as well!

**Don't justify failure.

While unsuccessful people keep cribbing about their growing age, their health problems, their poor time management, their lack of luck, their bosses and their lack of opportunities, successful people are busy finding ways to overcome their challenges.

On this note, read these words from Eleanor Roosevelt:

> "Great minds discuss ideas;
> Average minds discuss events;
> Small minds discuss people."

Believe in the beauty of your dreams.

*"Our Greatest Weakness Lies In Giving Up.
The Most Certain Way To Succeeed Is
Always To Try One More Time."*

- Thomas Edison

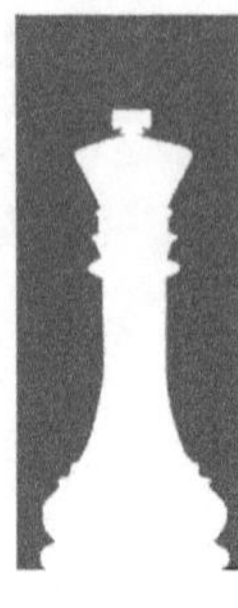

Chapter Two

ADDITIONAL VITAL THINGS YOU MUST KNOW AND DO TO BE A HIGH ACHIEVER

SUCCESS AND ACHIEVEMENTS IN LIFE ARE NOT DETERMINED JUST BY WHAT YOU HEAR or KNOW BUT WHAT YOU DO WITH WHAT YOU HEAR AND KNOW [Joshua 1:8].

Luke 11:28, *"But he said, Yea rather, blessed prosperous successful are they that hear the word of God, and keep (practise) it."*

Knowledge is not power; applied knowledge is power!

1. **Kill your excuses and procrastinations.** (Luke 14:16-18; 18-20)

Stop postponing things you must do today till tomorrow or the day after tomorrow. Do Matthew 6:33 now, not tomorrow. Be innovative and proactive! Pay now, play later; play now, pay a heavy price of regrets later. Everything in your life towards progress begins with prayer and doing the word so increase your word study life and prayer life by raising your prayer bar today not tomorrow.

PRAY HARD, STUDY HARD BUT WORK HARDER!!

Many of us are architects of our own destruction via procrastination, wrong words from our own lips and refusing to change.

What is Procrastination?

Procrastination is postponing what you must do today till tomorrow or the day after tomorrow.

*** PROCRASTINATION KILLS OPPORTUNITIES

"He who observes the wind will not sow, and he who regards the clouds will not reap" (Ecclesiastes 11:4)

ILLUSTRATION OF PROCRASTINATION:

A heavy rain had been falling as a man drove down a lonely road. As he rounded a curve, he saw an old farmer surveying the ruins of his barn. The driver stopped his car and asked what had happened. "Roof fell in," said the farmer. "Leaked so long it finally just rotted through."

"Why in the world didn't you fix it before it got that bad?" asked the stranger.

"Well, sir," replied the farmer, "it just seemed I never did get around to it. When the weather was good, there weren't no need for it, and when it rained, it was too wet to work on!" — Our Daily Bread.

Delaying to act always has negative consequences. A stitch in time saves nine. If we leave a problem for tomorrow, by tomorrow it may get bigger, even if our ability to tackle it remains the same.

The Bible says, *"Do not boast about tomorrow, for you do not know what a day may bring"* (Proverbs 27:1).

The best time to do what we should is now. Sometimes we delay because we are simply afraid, and in many cases the things we fear are not real. Then it gets too late and we lose grounds. The Bible says "Even though I walk through the darkest valley, I will fear no evil, for you are with me; your rod and your staff, they comfort me" (Psalm 23:4). Other causes of procrastination are laziness and distractions. Distractions make us carry out legitimate activities that have no direct bearing on our major goals.

2. Destroy every form of distraction.

Stay very focussed on what you want to achieve each year including knowing, familiarising yourself with and prioritising what God, your church and organisation wants to achieve with you and through you this year.

AVOID GOING IN TOO MANY DIRECTIONS!

Always feed your focus not your distractors or distractions. Focus on what you want to achieve and your intended destination not the distractions or distractors and time wasters. Not everyone at the bus stop, train station or airport is travelling.

Not everyone in school, college or university is there for a degree. So, stop asking for directions from them or engaging in elongated conversations with them. Your bus, train or airplane may take off without you. (Hebrews 12:1-2)

Distractions will never cease; we will continue to fight against them. We must wage war against our fears. We should resolve to start doing things before we are perfectly ready. As each day breaks, current problems get older, bigger and become more difficult (if not too late) to tackle.

3. **Avoid associating with negative and non-progressive minds** i.e. those allergic to progress and who are not good for your mental health.

This is simply because they have a problem with every solution. Associate with people who add to you and multiply you spiritually, mentally, intellectually, financially, physically and whom you can add to instead of those who subtract from you, drain you and divide you. If you want to become more spiritual, then associate with people who are more spiritual than you. If you want to be a blessing, associate with people who are already a blessing to others; if you want to become a better wife, associate with wives who are submissive to their husbands and help their husbands not those who are proud, insolent and who get their kicks from provoking their husbands to wrath. If you want to be a better husband, associate with husbands who love their wives as their own selves and give their lives for them. If you want to be an 'A' student, associate with 'A' students. In summary, if you want to be an achiever, associate with people who are Achievers not non-achievers!

BE SMART: "Share your creative ideas with an innovator and you will be on your way to building an empire. Share your ideas with one who has no aspirations for a better and successful life, they will find everything wrong with it, and eventually kill it." - Victor Kwegyir

Avoid toxic people and Proverbs 6:16-19 people. You cannot Finish Well hanging around these people.

Proverbs 6:16-19, *'These six things doth the Lord hate: yea, seven are an abomination unto him: A proud look, a lying tongue, and hands that shed innocent blood, An heart that deviseth wicked imaginations, feet that be swift in running to mischief, A false witness that speaketh lies, and he that soweth discord among brethren.'*

MAKE SURE YOUR BEST FRIENDS ARE PEOPLE WHO ARE MORE SPIRITUAL, BETTER, WISER, RICHER, HARDWORKING AND MORE INFLUENTIAL THAN YOU NOT THE OTHER WAY ROUND.

It is better to run with horses and be last than to be first in a race with tortoises. Who you keep company with is what determines what accompanies you. You will become who you hang out with often. So:

Stay clear of those who have nothing to lose.

To be an achiever, ALWAYS Hang out with and seek counsel from people who are wiser and more knowledgeable with proven results than you are. (Proverbs 11:14; 15:22; 24:6)

Surround yourself with those who bring out the best in you, not the stress in you.

Luke 2:46-49, 52, *"And it came to pass, that after three days they found him in the temple, sitting in the midst of the doctors, both hearing them, and asking them questions. And all that heard him were astonished at his understanding and answers. And when they saw him, they were amazed: and his mother said unto him, Son, why hast thou thus dealt with us? behold, thy father and I have sought thee sorrowing. And he said unto them, How is it that ye sought me? wist ye not that I must be about my Father's business?"*

YOU ARE EITHER SUBMITTING TO MENTORS OR TORMENTORS.

Without a role model, you can hardly play your role well.

"And Jesus increased in wisdom and stature, and in favour with God and man." - Luke 2:52

4. **Be totally addicted to self or personal development and intoxicated with spiritual and mental development as a lifestyle.**

BLIND MINDS ARE WORSE THAN BLIND EYES; ONLY THOSE WHO USE THEIR HEADS GO AHEAD IN LIFE;

Charles 'Tremendous' Jones said: You are the same person today that you will be in five years except for two things; the books you read and the people you associate with."

Every day, you Are Either Building A Library Or A Mortuary Without Knowing.

To be an achiever, ALWAYS Hang out with and seek counsel from achievers, people who are wiser and more knowledgeable with proofs and results than you are.

BETTER TO RUN WITH HORSES AND BE LAST THAN TO BE FIRST IN A RACE WITH TORTOISE.

Deuteronomy 34:9, JOSHUA HAD WISDOM BECAUSE MOSES LAID HANDS ON HIM!

Nothing happens by chance.

Hebrews 6:12, *"That ye be not slothful, but followers of them who through faith and patience inherit the promises."*

5. **Never let a day go past without knowing more, doing more, achieving more, becoming better than the day before.**

Proverbs 4:18, *"The path of the just is like the shining light, shining brighter and brighter [more and more] unto the perfect day."*

Abraham Lincoln said: 'I don't care much about anyone who is not wiser today than they were yesterday.'

Success in any endeavour including ministry consists of little daily efforts while failure consists of little daily neglects.

Henry Ford said: "<u>Anyone</u> who <u>stops</u> <u>learning</u> is old, <u>whether</u> at twenty or eighty. Anyone who keeps learning, stays young whether at twenty or eighty. The <u>greatest</u> <u>thing</u> in life is to keep your mind <u>young</u>."

6. Never stop learning. Be addicted to knowledge and wisdom acquisition.

One of our great capacities is the ability (and urge) to learn. Unfortunately, most of us stop actively learning once our formal education stops. We allow ourselves to remain stagnant in our careers and personal lives.

Jim Rohn said, 'Formal education will make you a living but self-education or continuous learning will make you a fortune.'

Dale Beaumont, once said, "If you are not green and growing, you are ripe and rotting."

Dr. David Oyedepo said: "You are either building a library or a mortuary without knowing."

Abraham Lincoln said, "I don't care much about anyone who is not wiser today than they were yesterday."

And Henry Ford said: "Anyone who stops learning is old, whether at twenty or eighty. Anyone who keeps learning stays young. The greatest thing in life is to keep your mind young.

YOU CANNOT KEEP YOUR MIND YOUNG AND FEEL OR LOOK OLD OR TIRED — never!

How much of your week do you dedicate to learning? Schooling is periodic but continuous learning is ongoing. Schooling gives you a certificate, but continuous learning makes you a fortune.

"Formal education will make you a living; self education will make you a fortune" – Jim Rohn

7. **Never do at noon (PM) what you should have done in the AM of your life and never do in the evenings of your life what you should have done in the AM OR NOON (PM or afternoon) of your life.**

THERE IS A TIME FOR EVERYTHING AND A SEASON FOR EVERY PURPOSE UNDER HEAVEN (Ecclesiastes 3:1-8).

BE very MINDFUL OF THE 3 or 4 stages of life and purpose like Daniel purposed in his heart (Daniel 1:8) to live your life on schedule or better still ahead of schedule.

8. **Network and Build mutual relationships with those who are already where you want to be and those who are more pregnant than you.**

Don't get complacent, content or satisfied with those who are behind you; rather be motivated and challenged by those who are far ahead of you.

Luke 1:41-44, *"When Elizabeth heard Mary's greeting, the baby leaped in her womb, and Elizabeth was filled with the Holy Spirit. In a loud voice she exclaimed: "Blessed are you among women, and blessed is the child you will bear! But why am I so favored, that the mother of my Lord should come to me? As soon as the sound of your greeting reached my ears, the baby in my womb leaped for joy."*

Ezekiel 2:2, *"And the spirit entered into me when he spake unto me, and set me upon my feet, that I heard him that spake unto me"*

John 6:63, *"It is the spirit that quickeneth; the flesh profiteth nothing: the words that I speak unto you, they are spirit, and they are life."*

If you have a dream, hang out with dreamers; if you have a vision, hang out with visionaries. If you have a desire to be successful, hang around success stories. If you have a goal, hang out with goal-setters, goal getters and goal-achievers. Be among those who will challenge you to do more, stretch you and guide you towards excellence, achievement and fulfilment in life. Remember: IRON SHARPENS IRON NOT WOOD. (Proverbs 27:17)

*Remember: A person who has nothing to lose will help you lose everything you've ever worked for.

9. Always feed your focus not your distractors or distractions.

There are distracters and distractions everywhere. Focus on what you want to achieve and your intended destination not the distractions, or distractors and time wasters. Winston Churchill is known to have said "You will never reach your destination if you stop and throw stones at every dog that barks"

Like I said earlier: Not everyone at the bus stop, train station or airport is travelling. Not everyone in school, college or university is there for a degree. So, stop asking for directions from them or engaging in elongated conversations with them or from people who are going nowhere or coming to see someone off or admire the train, tram, buses, plane or airport. Your bus, train or airplane may take off without you. Not everyone in church is there for God or others; some are there just for what to take or what to get I.e. just living for themselves and others are there to frustrate and destroy. Don't be naive.

NOT EVERYONE IN ZION IS FOR ZION!

Philippians 3:2, *"Beware of dogs, beware of evil workers, beware of the concision."*

Philippians 3:2, NASB: *"Beware of the dogs, beware of the evil workers, beware of the false circumcision."*

Their god is their bellies. Philippians 3:19, *"Whose end is destruction, whose god is their belly, and whose glory is in their shame, who mind earthly things.)"*

Remember: A person who has nothing to lose will help you lose everything you've ever worked for.

10. Be patient and consistent in what you do.

Don't give up too easily. Don't faint along the way or give up too easily. Remain constant. (Proverbs 24:10)

The key to success and achievements in God's kingdom is: WORK LIKE IT ALL DEPENDS ON YOU AND PRAY LIKE IT ALL DEPENDS ON GOD! Work like it all depends on you and pray like it all depends on God! Martin Luther the revivalist from Germany also the founder of the Lutherans said, 'I have held many things in my hands, and I have lost them all; but whatever you have placed in God's hand will allow you to fall flat on your face in order to get you on your knees.' If you're wise, you won't wait for that to happen.

To grow spiritually is to fully depend on God wholeheartedly. Dr. Mike Murdock said: "Your life will always move in the direction of your strongest thoughts. You create a season of good success every time you complete an instruction from God and your seasons of life will change every time you decide to use your faith."

Hebrews 12:1, *"Wherefore seeing we also are compassed about with so great a cloud of witnesses, let us lay aside every weight, and the sin which doth so easily beset us, and let us run with patience the race that is set before us."*

1 Timothy 1:18, *"This charge I commit unto thee, son Timothy, according to the prophecies which went before on thee, that thou by them mightest war a good warfare"*

1 Timothy 6:12, *"Fight the good fight of faith, lay hold on eternal life, whereunto thou art also called, and hast professed a good profession before many witnesses."*

2 Timothy 4:7, *"I have fought a good fight, I have finished my course, I have kept the faith"*

11. Commit yourself to Add value to people's lives.

Maintain a VAT [VALUE-ADDING TRAITS] lifestyle.

WIN AND LET OTHERS WIN TOO

Make a quality decision to Add value to people's lives daily by adding value to yourself daily i.e. spiritually, mentally, financially, physically, etc. Maintain a VAT lifestyle!

You are blessed to be a blessing (Genesis 12:1-3; 22:16-18) so, ask yourself questions like 'Am I growing spiritually or mentally?' because you can't give what you don't have.

"Carry each other's burdens, and in this way, you will fulfil the law of Christ" (Galatians 6:2)

"When one side benefits more than the other, that's a win-lose situation. To the winner it might look like success for a while, but in the long run, it breeds resentment and distrust" (Stephen Covey).

We cannot achieve greatness (not for a long time) if all we do is to show up to get everything we want. The goal should be to show up and give everything we have; that doesn't mean stripping ourselves of everything, but making sure we do not take it all.

"Greater love has no one than this: to lay down one's life for one's friends" (John 15:13). Win and let others win because everybody wants to win. There are many times in life when we should sacrifice so others can have their share of winning.

Think about other people's happiness and success; do that consistently enough, and you will have enough people willing to help you climb the ladder of success. You can't win every argument. You can't take all the good things in a business contract. Let your spouse win more often. Let your children win over you sometimes. Show your friends by your actions how much you care, and how much you can do for them and you will have more friends than you need to succeed. If others can't win with us, we will never be winners in the true sense of it.

The bible says, *"Not looking to your own interests, but each of you to the interests of the others"* (Philippians 2:4). Everyone should be given the chance to take something home. Sharing and caring breeds more success than tearing down others to get whatever we want. The best way may not be your own or the other person's way, the best way will most likely be the middle way, so, always meet people at the middle, and you will experience less trouble. The more people that win because of us, the more success we will enjoy in life.

"When you win, I win. We all win" — Unknown

"Let brotherly love continue" — Hebrews 13:1

"Let not mercy and truth forsake thee: bind them about thy neck; write them upon the table of thine heart: So shalt thou find favour and good understanding in the sight of God and man." - Proverbs 3:3-4

"Therefore, my beloved brethren, be ye stedfast, unmoveable, always abounding in the work of the Lord, forasmuch as ye know that your labour is not in vain in the Lord." — 1 Corinthians 15:58

Galatians 6:6-9 in summary says, *'...Never stop doing good irrespective...'*

12. Refuse to be stagnant, stale and archaic.

Learn new things every day that makes you look so stupid or ignorant yesterday. Refuse to be old in your mind, your thinking, and refuse to be stagnant, stale and archaic.

NEVER STAY IN ONE SPOT!

Remember: OLD or Aged DOESN'T ALWAYS MEAN WISE OR SENSIBLE!

"The illiterates of the 21st century are not those who cannot read or write but those who cannot learn, unlearn and relearn." — Alvin Toffler

Life is like a library; wisdom is the ability to know the right books to read (Jeremiah 1:15) and the right people to associate with.

Don't entertain people who poison you about your Pastors, coaches or mentors i.e. your life-source and church where you eat from and learn from. As Charles 'Tremendous' Jones said: 'You are the same person today that you will be in five years time except for two things; the books you read and the people you associate with [or keep as your constant company / companions]."

In life, you are either building a library or a mortuary without knowing. Every day, you are either heading in the direction of destiny or far away from it by the books you read and the people you keep company with. [Psalm 1:1-3; 1 Corinthians 15:33]

EMPHASIS: 'I do not think much of a man who is not wiser today that he was yesterday.' - Abraham Lincoln

"Anyone who stops learning is old, whether at twenty or eighty. Anyone who keeps learning stays young whether at twenty or eighty. The greatest thing in life is to keep your mind young". - Henry Ford.

13. Have a written goal or goals and clearly define your purpose and pursue it with all your might.

Personal goals, family goals, career goals, goals for your church and department, souls, seeds, prayer goals, bible study, time with

God, etc. What are your goals, targets you've set for yourself, your department in your church or your family?

"If you want to live a happy life, tie it to a goal not objects or people." — Albert Einstein

When you set a goal, it motivates you to start planning how to realise it.

What are the qualities you intend to teach, train and pass on to your children that those qualities don't die with you but your children live it and pass on that same legacy to the next generation? What are you teaching your children about God and God's House? We are all admonished to teach and train our children the following qualities. "Train up a child in the way he should go: and when he is old, he will not depart from it." (Proverbs 22:6)

"You can only teach your children to love God as much as you love Him." — MAMA B

Abraham qualified for God's secrets and became God's confidant through God's personal testimony of him in Genesis 18:17-19, that he would COMMAND HIS CHILDREN AND HOUSEHOLD AFTER HIM "And the Lord said, Shall I hide from Abraham that thing which I do; Seeing that Abraham shall surely become a great and mighty nation, and all the nations of the earth shall be blessed in him? For I know him, that he will command his children and his household after him, and they shall keep the way of the Lord, to do justice and judgment; that the Lord may bring upon Abraham that which he hath spoken of him."

14. **Commit yourself to a life of WORKING HARD AND WORKING SMART TO PROVIDE solutions and SOLVE problems IN YOUR FIELD OR CALLING and you will never lack.**

15. **Visualise where you want to be by the end of each year and at the end of your life and be ready to pay the required price to get there.**

How would you want to be remembered or WHAT DO YOU WANT TO BE REMEMBERED FOR IN LIFE IN GENERAL? AS A PROBLEM-SOLVER, IDLE OR A PROBLEM-CREATOR? A NUISANCE OR RELEVANT? GOSSIP OR GOSPEL PREACHER? POOR OR RICH? As a wandering generality or a meaningful specific? A Burden or a blessing? Problematic or a joy?

Note!!!

A lot of people will tell you something isn't going to work. It's your choice whether you listen to them or prove them wrong by pursuing your purpose and vision with laser-like focus, determination and dedication. GO FORWARD!

Remember: People who say it cannot be done are always interrupted by others doing it i.e. what they said cannot be done.

SO: DEFY PEOPLE'S OPINION and Remember: WHEN IT COMES TO YOUR DESTINY, MAJORITY DOES NOT CARRY THE VOTE; ONLY YOUR VOTE COUNTS! When it comes to your destiny, it's only what you know and what you do with what you know that COUNTS!

KNOWLEDGE IS NOT POWER; APPLIED KNOWLEDGE IS! Receive Great Grace to finish what you started in Jesus name.

16. Be Selective In What You Tolerate

WHATEVER YOU TOLERATE, YOU PERPETUATE.

Make up your mind that this year will end well for you. YOU WILL END THIS YEAR WELL!

Moses said to the nation, Israel, *"I have set before you life and death, blessing and cursing; therefore choose life that both thou and thy seed may live…"* [Deuteronomy 30:19]

The Bible says, *"I tell you the truth, whatever you forbid on earth will be forbidden in heaven, and whatever you permit on earth will be permitted in heaven"* (Matthew 18:18). If a person allows negative thinking to dominate their minds, they will be driven in a negative direction. If a person permits or lives with ignorance in any aspect of their lives, ignorance will take root in that particular area. If we allow people who habitually gossip to drag us into their baseless conversations, we will be influenced by the things they say.

ASSOCIATION RAISES OR ERAZES; ASSOCIATION ADDS OR SUBTRACTS: ASSOCIATION INCREASES OR DECREASES!

17. Do not ignore people who treat you the way you dislike or hate otherwise they will continue to treat you that way. Shut them down! Shut them out!

FRIENDSHIP IS BY CHOICE NOT BY FORCE!!

Life is so short we should not allow in our lives, things or people that do not lead us where we want to be or those who poison us about our LIFE-SOURCE i.e. Fathers, Mentors, Prophets and Pastors God has strategically placed in our lives. They are life-sources.

Fathers and Pastors are carriers of many graces and virtues and are given to us as assets i.e. additions and multipliers of destiny. They are life-sources and life-givers. Every time you obey and honour your Pastor, goodwill, wellbeing and long life flows from them toward you but every time you think of or plan evil, harbour or speak evil of or condone or entertain enemies of a life-source, you cut yourself off from receiving the life they carry from their reservoir for you. You lose, stagnate, decline and are eventually destroyed but they continue to move higher irrespective because they remain life-givers. They take what they carry where they are received and celebrated not tolerated. (John 1:12; Mark 6:2-6)

IF YOU CAN'T STAND OR SUBMIT TO A PASTOR YOU SIT UNDER, CHECK YOUR HEART OR LEAVE THAT CHURCH FOR YOUR SAKE NOT HIS SAKE!!! Whatever we condone will continue, and whatever we put up with will take roots. If we permit sickness, demons, diseases, pests and people to make our life unbearable, they will stay until we kick them out. The bible says, *"…submit to God, resist the devil and he will flee from you"* (James 4:7).

Never allow people to break your boundaries or violate you in any way, because they do not own your life. If you tolerate poverty, you will stay poor. If you accept that you are not capable of doing certain things, you will never grow beyond your present level.

There are things we should learn to tolerate in our lives because they will help to move us forward such as pain, discomfort, differences, risk-taking, smart hard work, exercise and healthy foods that we do not really like, because they are great for our lives but never tolerate anything or anyone that doesn't build you up or take you forward. Refuse to accommodate things and people that are contrary and allergic to God's Word, your pastor, your church, destiny and things and people that do not add to your life.

"You get what you tolerate." — Henry Cloud

18. Stop tolerating things and people whose behaviour and actions constantly aggravate your spirit and bring the worst out of you.

Stop entertaining things and people you don't like, who look down on you, whom you can't stand, who constantly upset you, provoke you, make you angry all the time, waste your time, use you and discard you or who always aggravate your spirit or bring the worst out of you.

19. Do not ignore, harbour or entertain people who dishonour or disrespect you, treat you the way you dislike or hate otherwise they will continue to treat you that way.

Shut them up and shut them down! Move them! SOME PEOPLE WILL BETTER YOUR LIFE BY BEING IN IT WHILE OTHERS WILL BETTER IT BY STAYING OUT! THERE ARE THOSE WHO BRING JOY WHEREVER THEY GO AND THOSE WHO BRING JOY WHENEVER THEY GO! You choose which one you are. There are people including Christians you must rebuke sharply and tell them they are wrong when they are wrong. Don't sympathise with them or you will soon be contaminated to think and behave like them, seeing things from their perspective.

Titus 1:10-13, *"For there are many unruly and vain talkers and deceivers, specially they of the circumcision: Whose mouths must be stopped, who subvert whole houses, teaching things which they ought not, for filthy lucre's sake. One of themselves, even a prophet of their own, said, The Cretians are alway liars, evil beasts, slow bellies. This witness is true. Wherefore rebuke them sharply, that they may be sound in the faith"*.

20. SET AND ENFORCE BOUNDARIES FOR YOUR LIFE AND DESTINY and Never allow people to break your focus, your boundaries or violate you or your principles in any way, shape or form because they do not own your life.

Remember: WHEN PURPOSE IS DISCOVERED, RELATIONSHIPS ARE TRIMMED!

SET AND ENFORCE YOUR PERSONAL BOUNDARIES

"Stand fast therefore in the Liberty wherewith Christ hath made us free..." (Galatians 5:1).

Personal boundaries help to define who you are i.e. your likes, dislikes and how close you want people to get to you. Anything goes where there are no boundaries. Paul admonished Timothy: *"Let no man despise thy youth; but be thou an example of the believers, in word, in conversation, in charity, in spirit, in faith, in purity"* (1 Timothy 4:12). We need to set boundaries for all aspects of our lives.

Don't stand as a surety or guarantor for anyone's bills, loans, higher purchase, insurance, mortgage or property.

Proverbs 11:15, *"He that is surety for a stranger shall smart for it; But he that hateth suretyship is secure."*

Proverbs 11:15 ESV, *"Whoever puts up security for a stranger will surely suffer harm, but he who hates striking hands in pledge is secure."*

Proverbs 11:15 ISV, *"Securing a loan for a stranger will bring suffering, but by refusing to do so, one remains safe."*

Proverbs 11:15 NIV, *"Whoever puts up security for a stranger will surely suffer, but whoever refuses to shake hands in pledge is safe."*

Decide whether you want to lend anyone your property, money or some other material. When you establish emotional boundaries, you will not allow others to play around with your feelings without your permission; you will not allow your emotions to be out of control. Don't allow people to just go in and out of your life, home or office without setting and maintaining boundaries.

King Ahab asked for a land that belonged to Naboth. *'And Naboth said to Ahab, The LORD forbid it me, that I should give the inheritance of my fathers unto thee.'* (1 Kings 21:3).

Naboth defended and died for his physical boundaries. We should not compromise our faith, prayer life, bible studies, church attendance or projects for anything. Protect your relationship with God, Your church and Pastor.

Let people know respectfully, where you stand. When you have healthy boundaries in place, you will not put people's needs before yours all the time; you will not let people take advantage of your kindness or generosity, and you will not yield to unhealthy pressures from others.

Setting boundaries may not be easy initially, but with time, respectfully and firmly insist on what you want and people will get to understand that they can only go so far with you. Be free to be yourself. We should all learn to respect other people's likes and dislikes. Setting boundaries does not make a person selfish; it means that they want us to know how far they are prepared to go.

Revelation 3:11, *'I am coming soon. Hold fast what you have, so that no one may seize your crown.'*

Daniel 3:16-18, *"Shadrach, Meshach, and Abednego, answered and said to the king, O Nebuchadnezzar, we are not careful to answer thee in this matter. If it be so, our God whom we serve is able to deliver us from the burning fiery furnace, and he will deliver us out of thine hand, O king. But if not, be it known unto thee, O king, that we will not serve thy gods, nor worship the golden image which thou hast set up."*

Acts 4:18-20, *"And they called them, and commanded them not to speak at all nor teach in the name of Jesus. But Peter and John answered and said unto them, Whether it be right in the sight of God to hearken unto you more than unto God, judge ye. For we cannot but speak the things which we have seen and heard."*

"When we fail to set boundaries and hold people accountable, we feel used and mistreated." — Brene Brown

21. Drop these seemingly 'Harmless' Habits or Quit doing things that hinder your success, such as:

A. Not Prioritizing Your Day: Start using A Daily or Weekly Productivity Planner; it will change everything for you. It forces you to actually sit down and only pick a few things you're going to get done, especially the things that often end up getting undone from day to day. Do not let Your calendar and to-do list run your day where you never feel like you are getting the important things done. Major on majors and minor on minors.

B. Saying 'Yes' When You Actually Want to Say 'No' To People.

If a project, partnership or opportunity doesn't resonate with you and does not feel aligned with your values, destiny and your goals, you need to be comfortable about setting boundaries. Learn how to say no with kindness right from the start because, as you become more successful, more people will compete for your time and attention. Not setting healthy boundaries will end up overwhelming you and you suffering burnout after people have used you and discarded you. ****WHEN PURPOSE IS DISCOVERED, RELATIONSHIPS ARE TRIMMED!****FRIENDSHIP IS BY CHOICE NOT BY FORCE!

C. Hanging On To People Who Refuse To or Don't Want to Change, Grow or Develop

Stop Hanging On To People Who Refuse To or Don't Want to Change, Grow or Develop.

For leaders, pastors and business owners especially, the people who got your company or ministry to where you are today may not be the ones to get you to where you want to be tomorrow. If they can't grow with you, and refuse to attend group Prayer, ministry or company training and to undertake self or personal development and improvement sessions, at their own expense, it's time to replace them with those who can.

D. Forcing Your Help On People Who Don't Need, Appreciate or Want Your Help.

Stop Forcing Your Help On People Who Don't Need, Appreciate or Want Your Help; Let them ask for it When They Are Desperate For it.

E. Assuming everyone around you is for you or loyal to you.

Don't assume everyone around you is for you or loyal to you. Some people's loyalty to you ends the moment their need of you ends and they find another person who provides or meets that need in their life.

F. Entering relationships with your head first instead of your heart.

Not Defining Relationships And Expectations Clearly And In Detail By Making Assumptions And Having Unrealistic Expectations Can Break Your Heart And Lead To Irreparable Damages/Illnesses

ENTER RELATIONSHIPS WITH YOUR HEAD (Divine Wisdom And Common Sense) FIRST BEFORE YOUR HEART, BEFORE YOU END UP LIVING A LIFE FULL OF REGRETS. LET YOUR HEART FOLLOW YOUR HEAD NOT THE OTHER WAY ROUND!

G. Being Committed To People Who Are Not Committed or Wholeheartedly Contributory To You or Your Cause.

This can be devastating.

Never become committed to anything or anyone who is not wholeheartedly committed to you or your cause. John 2:24-25, *"But Jesus did not commit himself unto them, because he knew all men, And needed not that any should testify of man: for he knew what was in man."*

Matthew 10:37, *"Anyone who loves their father or mother more than me is not worthy of me; anyone who loves their son or daughter more than me is not worthy of me."*

PUZZLE: Romans 15:27, *"It hath pleased them verily; and their debtors they are. For if the Gentiles have been made partakers of their spiritual things, their duty is also to minister unto them in carnal things."*

Proverbs 27:23-27, *"Be thou diligent to know the state of thy flocks, and look well to thy herds. For riches are not for ever: and doth the crown endure to every generation? The hay appeareth, and the tender grass sheweth itself, and herbs of the mountains are gathered. The lambs are for thy clothing, and the goats are the price of the field. And thou shalt have goats' milk enough for thy food, for the food of thy household, and for the maintenance for thy maidens."*

Pastors have Done so much for members but members do so little for them or give so little to them and the church from the much they received as fruits from the care and teachings from the pulpit.

Deuteronomy 14:27, *"And do not neglect the Levites living in your towns, for they have no allotment or inheritance of their own."*

1 Corinthians 9:8-14, *"Say I these things as a man? or saith not the law the same also? For it is written in the law of Moses, Thou shalt not muzzle the mouth of the ox that treadeth out the corn. Doth God take care for oxen? Or saith he it altogether for our sakes? For our sakes, no doubt, this is written: that he that ploweth should plow in hope; and that he that thresheth in hope should be partaker of his hope. If we have sown unto you spiritual things, is it a great thing if we shall reap your carnal things? If others be partakers of this power over you, are not we rather? Nevertheless we have not used this power; but suffer all things, lest we should hinder the gospel of Christ. Do*

ye not know that they which minister about holy things live of the things of the temple? and they which wait at the altar are partakers with the altar? Even so hath the Lord ordained that they which preach the gospel should live of the gospel."

Provide Meat In God's House: Malachi 3:8-12

22. Be careful about who you give permission or license to make deposits into your life and withdrawals from your life.

Remember: If you allow people to make more withdrawals than deposits in your life, you will soon be out of balance, in deficit and in the negative. Know when to close the account with speed swiftly.

Some claim allegiance or loyalty to you but are actually in your life not to add to you but for what to get from you. They are not loyal to you because their so-called loyalty to you ends once their need of you ends. Shine your eyes!!

23. Don't keep people around who don't appreciate you and think they are doing you a favour by being there.

Stop entertaining or pampering people who think they are doing you a favour by being in your life, business or ministry.

You were blessed before they showed up! YOU HAD A PURPOSE BEFORE ANYONE HAD AN OPINION!!! GOD HAD A PURPOSE AND A PLAN FOR YOUR LIFE LONG BEFORE THEY SHOWED UP IN YOUR LIFE.

Jeremiah 29:11, *"For I know the thoughts that I think toward you, saith the Lord, thoughts of peace, and not of evil, to give you an expected end."*

Proverbs 19:21, *"There are many devices in a man's heart; nevertheless (only) the counsel of the Lord, that shall stand."*

24. Don't share your inner thoughts, valuable time or secrets with people who just tolerate you. GO AND SHARE YOUR SUCCESS SECRETS WHERE YOU ARE CELEBRATED NOT WHERE YOU ARE TOLERATED! (To young ministers, don't leave a ministry prematurely quoting the above statement: Instead, Endure hardness and finish your training there).

25. Stop allowing people who do so little for you to control so much of your mind, feelings and emotions. Shut that door and Don't let them in anymore.

Reason: A negative mind will never give you a positive life!

Don't let small minds convince you that your dreams are too big.

SMALL MINDS DISCUSS PEOPLE, AVERAGE MINDS DISCUSS EVENTS BUT GREAT MINDS DISCUSS IDEAS AND IT IS IDEAS THAT RULE THE WORLD!

26. Stop making a living and start making a difference.

In life, you are either making a living or making a difference.

A MEANINGFUL LIFE IS BY DESIGN NOT BY DEFAULT!

If you don't design your own life plan, chances are you will fall into someone else's plan and guess what they've got planned for you. Not much!!

As Jim Rohn said: "We all have two choices: We can make a living or we can design a life."

DESIGN YOUR LIFE!

27. Step out of your comfort zone and do something new and different.

Until you are ready to be different, you will never make a difference and until you leave your present shores you will Never discover new lands or territories, know what you are really capable of and maximise your full potential. IF YOU DON'T LIVE ON THE EDGE, YOU WILL NEVER SEE THE VIEW! So, step out!

It is true that achievers and successful people have fears, doubts, and worries; but they just don't let those feelings stop them. They don't give up. They go the extra mile until they achieve their goals, ambitions, aspirations and success.

28. Stop disliking people, avoiding people or relating with people from what someone told you about them.

Carry out your own investigations and get to know people for yourself. Know and relate with people both by discernment and by what you know personally about them. Know no man in the flesh but in the spirit (2 Corinthians 5:16). Even Jesus had to ask His disciples, 'Who do men [others] say I am… Who do you say I am?' (Matthew 16:13-15)

In other words, relate with me by your personal revelation of me not by what someone said.

Matthew 16:13-17, *"When Jesus came to the region of Caesarea Philippi, he asked his disciples, "Who do people say the Son of Man is?" They replied, "Some say John the Baptist; others say Elijah; and still others, Jeremiah or one of the prophets." "But what about you?" he asked. "Who do you say I am?" Simon Peter answered, "You are the Messiah, the Son of the living God. Jesus replied, "Blessed are you, Simon son of Jonah, for this was not revealed to you by flesh and blood, but by my Father in heaven.""*

John 4:39-42, "Many of the Samaritans from that town believed in him because of the woman's testimony, "He told me everything I ever did." So when the Samaritans came to him, they urged him to stay with them, and he stayed two days. And because of his words many more became believers. They said to the woman, "We no longer believe just because of what you said; now we have heard for ourselves, and we know that this man really is the Savior of the world."**

29. DON'T ENTERTAIN FAILURE IN YOUR THOUGHTS.

Think only right and productive thoughts, because, YOU ARE WHAT YOU THINK!

Proverbs 23:7, *"For [as] a man thinketh in his hearty, so is he:…"*

Proverbs 21:5, *"The thoughts of the diligent tend only to plenteousness; but of every one that is hasty only to want."*

"You keep him in perfect peace whose mind is stayed on you…" (Isaiah 26:3).

Remember: Failure is more of a state of mind than lack of resources and the adverse circumstances that surround you.

A well-known tightrope walker had been performing at various levels in his career. According to him, "My whole life is high-wire walking". As he was walking on the wire one day, he plunged many feet to his death. His wife later said, "All he thought about for three months before, was falling." This man had been filling his mind previously with positive thoughts, but the moment he switched to negative thinking, things went disastrously wrong. What we feed our mind is what we get from life.

Negative and pessimistic thinking will produce negative and defeated lives. This tight-rope walker had been having success with the sport until he allowed his mind to go in the wrong direction. Like Peter in Luke 5:1-10, He started expecting the worst to happen, looking on the glooming and dark side of things i.e. the boisterous winds. No matter how good and able a person is, if they continually entertain negative thoughts about themselves, other people or anything for that matter, they will start to live out whatever they feed their minds. That's why Paul said in Ephesians 4:23-24, "be renewed in the spirit of your mind; …put on the new man, which after God is created in righteousness and true holiness"

Dr. Mike Murdock said: "Your life will always move in the direction of your strongest thoughts. You create a season of good success every time you complete an instruction from God and your seasons of life will change every time you decide to use your faith."

When people harbour failure, they will end up as failures. People who give room to bitterness will manifest vengeance and hatred; those who fill their lives with hope will feel and reap the results of hope. Negative thinking is the greatest obstacle to success any one can contend with. That's why Bible says "Finally, my brethren, whatsoever things are true, whatsoever things are honest, whatsoever things are just, whatsoever things are pure… if there be any virtue, and if there be any praise, think on these things" (Philippians 4:8).

When a person replaces negative thoughts with positive ones and acts accordingly, they will begin to have positive results. Begin and end each day with positive thoughts, no matter what the day throws at you.

Negative thinking finds reasons why things cannot be done, while positive thinking searches for reasons why things can be done.

2 Timothy 1:7, "For God has not given us the spirit of fear [or timidity] but of power love and a sound mind;"

"A negative attitude drains, a positive attitude energises." - Lindsey Rietzsch

30. Stay faithful, steadfast, resilient, loyal and committed in all you set your mind to do including what belongs to others.

REASON: Because: If You Fail The Test of Faithfulness, You Cannot Occupy Your High Place in Life! (Matthew 25:14-30).

Success or Achievement is not about a Change of place, location or an environment but a Change of Mind.

You can be in the desert and yet make Impact. John the Baptist located his ministry or church in the wilderness and still made it in the desert or bush eating locust and wild honey (John 1:23) without designer suits. Noble people left the city and came to look for him to get baptised in the bush. It's not a mistake to find yourself in your country, family or church. It is rather an opportunity for you to make Impact. Your background has nothing to do with your Success, Achievement or Failure. It is a Choice.

Oprah Winfrey is known to have said: EXCELLENCE IS THE GREATEST DETERRENT TO SEXISM AND RACISM.

Don't fail your Generation. God is counting on you. Receive Grace to influence and Make Impact and impart into lives in Jesus Mighty Name. It's time to learn, unlearn and relearn.

31. Avoid hesitation where you must be proactive.

HESITATION STEALS OPPORTUNITIES

"So He said to me, 'This is the Word of the LORD to Zerubbabel: Not by might nor by power, but by my Spirit, says the LORD Almighty" (Zechariah 4:6).

"My procrastination which has held me back was born of fear… now I know that to conquer fear I must always act without hesitation and the flutters in my heart will vanish. Now I know that action reduces the lion of terror… I will walk where the failure fears to walk." – Og Mandino

A moment of hesitation can lead to a lifetime of regrets. [2]

A moment of hesitation can lead to a lifetime of regrets.

"20 years from now you will be more disappointed by the things that you didn't do than by the ones you did do. So, throw off the bowlines. Sail away from the safe harbour. Catch the trade winds in your sails. Explore. Dream. Discover." – Mark Twain

"There is only one thing that makes a dream impossible to achieve: the fear of failure." – Paulo Coelho

Hesitation is a dream killer, opportunity thief and a joy stealer. We must learn not to hesitate in the face of opportunities. Do not hesitate to begin your race, and do not hesitate to finish the race. Ask God for the courage to take risks without being stopped by imaginary lions [*3] or consequences of failure. Even the best of athletes can lose a race because of a moment's hesitation.

The prophet Isaiah said in Isaiah 54:2-3, *"Enlarge the place of your tent, stretch your tent curtains wide, do not hold back; lengthen your chords, strengthen your stakes. For you will spread out to the right hand and to the left…"*

John F. Kennedy said: "Once you say you're going to settle for second, that's what happens to you in life…"

The thought of trying things outside our scope and resources can be frightening and crippling, but the bible says, *"I can do all things through Christ who strengthens me."* (Philippians 4:13). Do something scary every day; it is the only path to growth.

REMEMBER: NOAH LOOKED LIKE AN IDIOT UNTIL IT STARTED TO RAIN.

For many people reading this, hesitation has probably 'stolen' so much from you; the only way to avoid further pain and regrets is to start doing things you fear. Failure may embarrass you, but it won't kill you. Refuse to be held back by anything. Think big and act big, and if you fail, you know at least, you have tried.

"And the trouble is, if you don't risk anything, you risk even more" - Erica Jong.

32. Forget and learn from your negative past.

Remember: No matter how dirty and bad your past is, your future is spotless and flawless.

So, ignore the past and focus mainly on your future because it's brighter.

"The future belongs to those who believe in the beauty of their dreams" – Eleanor Roosevelt.

33. Believe in who and what God has made you and in the beauty of your dreams.

NO ONE CAN MAKE YOU FEEL INFERIOR WITHOUT YOUR CONSENT!

The following is a story about a battle of wits between Mahatma Gandhi and Professor Peters: It is said that: When Mahatma Gandhi was studying Law at the University College, London, a white professor, whose last name was Peters, disliked him intensely. One day, Mr. Peters was having lunch at the dining room when Gandhi came along with his tray and sat next to the professor. [*4]

The professor said,

"Mr. Gandhi, you do not understand, a pig and a bird do not sit together to eat." Gandhiji looked at him as a parent would a rude child and calmly replied, "You do not worry professor. I'll fly away," and he went and sat at another table. Mr. Peters, reddened with rage, decided to take revenge.

The next day in Class, he posed the following question: "Mr. Gandhi, if you were walking down the street and found a package, and within was a bag of wisdom and another bag with money, which one would you take?" Without hesitating, Gandhiji responded, "The one with the money, of course." Mr. Peters, smiling sarcastically said, "I, in your place, would have taken the wisdom." Mahatma Gandhi shrugged and responded, "Each one takes what he doesn't have."
Mr. Peters, by this time was fit to be tied. So great was his anger that he wrote on Mahatma Ghandi's exam sheet the word "IDIOT" and gave it to Gandhi. Gandhi took the exam sheet and sat down at his desk trying very hard to remain calm while he contemplated his next move. A few minutes later, Mahatma Gandhiji got up, went to the professor and told him in a dignified polite tone, "Mr. Peters, you signed the sheet, but you did not give me the grade."

Don't mess with intelligent people. This was a person who knew the power of self-discovery and adhered to the scripture in James 1:19, *"Be quick to hear, slow to speak and slow to anger."*

NO ONE CAN MAKE YOU FEEL INFERIOR WITHOUT YOUR CONSENT!

If people think you are stupid, don't leave them in no doubt by opening your mouth to speak and confirm what they were thinking. Always outthink thinkers and outwit those who think they are wiser than you.

34. Stay in the Word and paint your pictures from the Scriptures.

2 Corinthians 3:18, *"But we all, with open face beholding as in a glass the glory of the Lord, are changed into the same image from glory to glory, even as by the Spirit of the Lord."*

35. Prioritise time management and prioritise priorities only.

Foolish people waste time, average people spend time but wise people invest time. Foolish people discuss people, average people discuss events while wise and successful people and achievers discuss ideas.

Wisdom speaking through King Solomon in Proverbs 8:15 said: *"By me kings reign and rulers issue decrees that are just;"*

Also: Foolish people waste money, average people spend money but wise people invest money. Time-Management is crucial. In life, you are either investing time, marking time or wasting time. Every time wasted on frivolities is destiny wasted.

36. Follow your passion with determination and dedication and turn your passion into your profession.

Achievers are Purpose, Principle and Passion-Driven. Have a passion for success.

37. Ask for the seven spirits of God to manifest in your life and career and ministry to put you in a different class from others.

Isaiah 11:1-3, *"And there shall come forth a rod out of the stem of Jesse, and a Branch shall grow out of his roots: And the spirit of the Lord shall rest upon him, the spirit of wisdom and understanding, the spirit of counsel and might, the spirit of knowledge and of the fear of the Lord; And shall make him of quick understanding in the fear of the Lord: and he shall not judge after the sight of his eyes, neither reprove after the hearing of his ears:"*

The spirit of power, ability to become, produce and perform, the spirit of wisdom which is the spirit of excellence as Daniel exhibited in Daniel 6:2 to become a distinguished administrator. Excellence is the greatest deterrent to racism, sexism and tribalism. Pray for the spirit of understanding which is the spirit of intelligence to come up with divine ideas.

Job 32:8, *"BUT THERE IS A SPIRIT IN MAN AND THE INSPIRATION OF THE ALMIGHTY GIVETH THEM UNDERSTANDING."*

It empowers you to know where you belong and know what to do.

Luke 4:18-19 *"The Spirit of the LORD is on me, because he has anointed me to proclaim good news to the poor. He has sent me to proclaim freedom for the prisoners and recovery of sight for the blind, to set the oppressed free, to proclaim the year of the LORD's favor."*

Luke 21:15, *"For I will give you words and wisdom that none of your adversaries will be able to resist or contradict."*

38. INSIST ON AND TAKE BACK WHAT IS RIGHTFULLY YOURS THROUGH PRAYER AND SPIRITUAL WARFARE

Desperate Situations Require or Demand Desperate Measures [Matthew 11:12; 18:18-20; 16:16-20; 1 Corinthians 16:9]

LIFE DOES NOT GIVE YOU WHAT YOU DESERVE; LIFE ONLY GIVES YOU WHAT YOU DISCOVER IS RIGHTFULLY YOURS AND INSIST ON AND DEMAND THROUGH PRAYER AND HARD WORK! (READ Matthew 11:12; Deuteronomy 2:24)

In this kingdom, Only the desperate are entitled to empowerment and change of story; it takes a sincere desperation for you to enjoy true empowerment and to secure your inheritance. IN THIS KINGDOM NOTHING HAPPENS BY CHANCE. [2

Corinthians 10:4-6; FIGHT THE GOOD FIGHT OF FAITH LAY HOLD ... 1 Timothy 6:12].

THE BATTLE FOR THE FUTURE [MOSES and JESUS (babies) Joseph's brothers, David and king Saul].

'The two most important days in your life are the day you were born and the day you find out why.' - Mark Twain

Life is like a battlefield. In life you will meet people who bless and build and those who destroy and tear down; When God wants to bless you, He puts a person in your life. When Satan wants to destroy you, he also puts a person in your life. Wisdom is the ability to know or knowing who sent who.

Life is a battlefield not a play field.

Life is not a fun fare but warfare.

Life is not a playground but a battleground.

To finish well you must Fight for what's rightfully yours! Remember: not everyone you meet or who comes into your life has good intentions, means well or has your interest at heart - discern!

EXAMPLES:

Ezekiel 11:1-3, *"Then the Spirit lifted me up and brought me to the gate of the house of the LORD that faces east. There at the entrance of the gate were twenty-five men, and I saw among them*

Jaazaniah son of Azzur and Pelatiah son of Benaiah, leaders of the people. The LORD said to me, "Son of man, these are the men who are plotting evil and giving wicked advice in this city. They say, 'Haven't our houses been recently rebuilt? This city is a pot, and we are the meat in it."

Psalm 41:5-6, *"Mine enemies speak evil of me, When shall he die, and his name perish? When one of them comes to see me, he speaks falsely, while his heart gathers slander; then he goes out and spreads it around."*

1. Jabez - 1 Chronicles 4:9-10

2. Jacob - Genesis 32:26-28, *"And Jacob was left alone; and there wrestled a man with him until the breaking of the day. And when he saw that he prevailed not against him, he touched the hollow of his thigh; and the hollow of Jacob's thigh was out of joint, as he wrestled with him. And he said, Let me go, for the day breaketh. And he said, I will not let thee go, except thou bless me. And he said unto him, What is thy name? And he said, Jacob. And he said, Thy name shall be called no more Jacob, but Israel: for as a prince hast thou power with God and with men, and hast prevailed."*

3. Blind Bartimaeus - Mark 10:46-52

4. Woman with issue of blood - Mark 5:25-34 ****UNTIL YOU ARE SICK AND TIRED OF BEING SICK AND TIRED, YOU WON'T BE FREE AND YOU WILL REMAIN SICK AND TIRED.

5. Man sick of the palsy and his 4 crazy friends - Mark 2:1-12 (your faith is seen or made obvious by the corresponding steps you take to back what you believe)

6. Syrophoenician woman - Mark 7:24-30. The lesson is don't give up; rather plead your case and bring your strong reasons why you qualify for what you are asking. [Isaiah 41:21; 43:26]

7. Hezekiah - 2 Chronicles 32:24; Isaiah 38:1-8; I shall not die - Psalm 118:17; Pleading your case via Word-based promises and Prayer changes God's mind or reverses his previous decisions including death sentences [Isaiah 41:21; 43:26; Hezekiah - Isaiah 38:1-5]

    Prayer does not only change situations; it changes you first! WHAT HAVE THE DOCTORS OR HOME OFFICE SAID? How do you counter it? Service Record: Dorcas, Roman centurion.

8. Pursue overtake recover all — 1 Samuel 30:8

9. Prodigal son - I am going back — Luke 15:17

    That's why I said:

    ***Reaction to the present is what creates the future.

    ***Your Violent reaction to your present condition is what creates your desired outcome for the future — Isaiah 62

10. Joshua and Caleb - Numbers 13:30

11. Isaac entreats the Lord for his wife who was barren for 20 years despite the prophecy of her being a mother of thousands of thousands - Genesis 24/25

12. One thing that changed in Esau's life when he discovered his brother had stolen his blessing was when he was told 'when you get restless you can break the yoke off your neck' - Genesis 27:40; *"Isaac said to him, You'll live far from Earth's bounty, remote from Heaven's dew. You'll live by your sword, hand-to-mouth, and you'll serve your brother. But when you can't take it any more, you'll break loose (from Your anger and hatred) and run free."* - Genesis 27:39-40 MSG

    "You will live by the sword and you will serve your brother. But when you grow restless, you will throw his yoke from off your neck."" - Genesis 27:40 NIV

    RESULT OF RESTLESSNESS Genesis 33:1&9, NLT *"Then Jacob looked up and saw Esau coming with his 400 men....But Esau said, "I already have plenty, my brother. Keep what you have for yourself."* - Isaiah 59:19; Psalm 24:7-9.

13. Jonah said I've had enough of languishing in the belly of a fish - Jonah 1/2 Prayed and thanked God and the big fish released him fulfilling Philippians 4:6-9

14. Ezekiel 11 - prophesy against the conspirators, devisers of mischief at your gate.

15. Peter in Prison - *"Peter therefore was kept in prison: but prayer was made without ceasing of the church unto God for him. And when Herod would have brought him forth, the same night Peter was sleeping between two soldiers, bound with two chains: and the keepers before the door kept the prison. And, behold, the angel of the Lord came upon him, and a light shined in the prison: and he smote Peter on the side, and raised him up, saying, Arise up quickly. And his chains fell off from his hands."* - Acts 12:5-7

16. Paul and Silas - Acts 16:16-40 release earthquakes of deliverance in prison via prayer and Praise.

17. David with national plague - 2 Samuel 24:24

18. Roman centurion's servant in Luke 7:1-10 because he won't give up.

19. The church refused to allow Dorcas to stay dead because she was a giver and an asset to the church in Acts 9:36-42, "Now there was at Joppa a certain disciple named Tabitha, which by interpretation is called Dorcas: this woman was full of good works and almsdeeds which she did. And it came to pass in those days, that she was sick, and died: whom when they had washed, they laid her in an upper chamber. And forasmuch as Lydda was nigh to Joppa, and the disciples had heard that Peter was there, they sent unto him two men, desiring him that he would not delay to come to them. Then Peter arose and went with them. When he was come, they

brought him into the upper chamber: and all the widows stood by him weeping, and shewing the coats and garments which Dorcas made, while she was with them. But Peter put them all forth, and kneeled down, and prayed; and turning him to the body said, Tabitha, arise. And she opened her eyes: and when she saw Peter, she sat up. And he gave her his hand, and lifted her up, and when he had called the saints and widows, presented her alive. And it was known throughout all Joppa; and many believed in the Lord."

20. Importunity Prayers - Luke 11:8-10

21. David would not tolerate Goliath's defying of the armies of Israel in 1 Samuel 17. Turned national plague around through sacrifice.

39. BE AN ATMOSPHERE-CHANGER

While others are maintaining the status quo of being atmosphere-maintainers or atmosphere-polluters, you go ahead and change atmospheres.

<u>ATMOSPHERE-CHANGERS</u>

YOU BECOME AN ATMOSPHERE-CHANGER!

ACHIEVERS ARE ATMOSPHERE-CHANGERS.

When they enter an atmosphere, environment or climate, the place changes to suit or line up with their dictates, demeanour, command, countenance and current. Even dry grounds become fertile and wet ground when they step on it. For example: Jacob and Joseph in Laban and Potiphar's house in Genesis 30:27-30 and Genesis 39. When a covenant-practising person enters a place, house, ground, company or business, it changes for better. They are highly employable people and rarely and highly 'unsackable' and 'undismissable'.

Genesis 30:27, *"...And Laban said unto him, I pray you, if I have found favour in your eyes, tarry [or stay]: for I have learned by experience that the LORD has blessed me for your sake [or because of you or because of your presence]."*

Here in this chapter was Laban, an employer begging the employee to stay because he was an organisational asset and generational asset not an organisational or generational liability because of Proverbs 10:22.

The blessing of the LORD ON A PERSON OR A PLACE MAKETH RICH AND WEALTHY WITH NO SORROW ADDED.

You either carry it or you don't carry it and you cannot carry it and not know it; this is far beyond I gave money and got money back or I gave and I received [Luke 6:38]. **RATHER, YOU ARE A FERTILIZER THAT FERTILIZES PLACES YOU GO AND PEOPLE YOU MEET!!**

I said: You are a fertiliser that fertilises places you go and people you meet.

Not everyone calls and God answers.

Don't make that mistake. IT'S NOT EVERYONE'S PRAYER THAT GOD ANSWERS!

Psalm 20:1-5, *"May the LORD answer you when you are in distress; may the name of the God of Jacob protect you. May he send you help from the sanctuary and grant you support from Zion. May he remember all your sacrifices and accept your burnt offerings. May he give you the desire of your heart and make all your plans succeed. May we shout for joy over your victory and lift up our banners in the name of our God. May the LORD grant all your requests."*

LISTEN: In Psalm 20:1-5, verse 1&2 is because of vs.3.

So, the question is: What have you done for God that touched God to act or move on your behalf to answer you promptly?

EXAMPLES:

In 1 Kings 3, Verse 5-14 was because of verse 3-4.

Cornelius and his memorial offering in Acts 10:4 is what triggered an apostolic visitation.

It was the sacrifice in 2 Samuel 24:24-25 that triggered the end of the national plague.

In Luke 7:1-10 it was verse 4-5 that triggered verse 6-10.

In Mark 14:3-19, it was the service rendered to Jesus and the precious seed of the woman with the expensive alabaster ointment that made her a memorial.

In Genesis 22, it was Abraham's sacrifice of his only promised son, the one he loved that provoked the ears of God and answers to prayer.

In Daniel 12:3, you become a star by pointing many to righteousness.

In Genesis 8:20-21, God smelt a sweet savour after a sacrifice. Then *"Noah built an altar to the LORD and, taking some of all the clean animals and clean birds, he sacrificed burnt offerings on it. The LORD smelled the pleasing aroma and said in his heart: "Never again will I curse the ground because of humans, even though every inclination of the human heart is evil from childhood. And never again will I destroy all living creatures, as I have done."*

ONE MAN'S SACRIFICE WHOM WE DID NOT KNOW RESULTED IN GOD PROMISING NEVER TO DESTROY THE EARTH EVER AGAIN WITH A FLOOD.

In Psalm 126, it is those who sow in tears who reap in joy and it is those who go forth 'and weeping' bearing precious not common seed who doubtless return with their sheaves or harvest in their hands.

NOTHING COMES FREE IN THIS KINGDOM!!

IN THE WORLD, WEALTH IS AN ACQUISITION i.e. is ACQUIRED BUT, IN THIS KINGDOM, WEALTH IS AN ENTRUSTMENT i.e. it is ENTRUSTED or GIVEN TO PEOPLE WHO CAN BE TRUSTED TO MANAGE WELL A FEW.

Luke 16:10-11, *"He that is faithful in that which is least is faithful also in much: and he that is unjust in the least is unjust also in much. If therefore ye have not been faithful in the unrighteous mammon, who will commit to your trust the true riches?"*

NIV

"Whoever can be trusted with very little can also be trusted with much, and whoever is dishonest with very little will also be dishonest with much."

NLT

"If you are faithful in little things, you will be faithful in large ones. But if you are dishonest in little things, you won't be honest with greater responsibilities."

Philippians 4:19 is because of Philippians 4:15-18.

In Psalm 50, verse 15 happens when verse 14 is done *"...offer unto God thanksgiving and pay thy vows then call on me" [vs. 15] "in the day of trouble and I will deliver you"*.

FACT: It is not everyone who calls on God in the day of trouble and he hears them.

Don't waste your life because when it comes to the challenges of life, they don't serve notice.

Life is a battlefield not a play ground; you can win in the fight if you know God and he knows you and hears you; there is a category of people who before they call, He answers while they are yet speaking.

Isaiah 65:24, *"Before they call I will answer; while they are still speaking I will hear."*

This is because God knows them as covenant-practitioners and highly sacrificial people.

THEM THAT DO KNOW THEIR GOD, SHALL BE STRONG AND DO EXPLOITS [Daniel 11:32].

WHAT ARE THE BENEFITS?

Divine insurance coverage and security of life and resources including your relatives [Genesis 14:14-end]. They are covered by the covenant-keeper because He protects what He gives.

40. Start and remain OPTIMISTIC WHILE OTHERS ARE being PESSIMISTIC.

AN OPTIMIST SEES BLESSING IN EVERY CRISIS!

AN OPTIMIST FINDS FORTUNE IN EVERY MISFORTUNE!

An optimist sees advantage in every disadvantage.

Lesson: Use every disadvantage to your advantage!!!

"For God has not given us the spirit of fear and timidity, but of power, love and self-control" (2 Timothy 1:7).

A couple had a set of male twins. One of them was an incurable optimist, and the other was a chronic pessimist. The parents worried about the extreme behaviours of both children and decided to take them to a psychologist for help. The psychologist promised to help but did something unusual. With the parents' consent he placed the pessimistic child in a room full of toys so he can enjoy himself, and the optimist, he placed in a room that was filled with manure. They observed both boys through one-way mirrors. They observed that the pessimist complained that he had no one to play with, whilst the optimist, though in a stinking room full of manure, was observed digging through the manure. When asked why he dug through the manure, he replied saying with so much manure in the room, he was certain that there would be a little horse somewhere in that room. – Source Unknown

An optimist takes responsibility in every crisis, but a pessimist sees crisis in every responsibility. Challenges are inevitable in the Christian life. Job went through uncommon crisis. Yet, "In all this, Job sinned not, nor charged God foolishly." (Job 1:22). Keep praying; stop blaming; pray until you are out of the woods. Keep looking for something that will work. Habakkuk said: *"Although the fig tree shall not blossom, neither shall fruit be in the vines; the labour of the olives shall fail … yet I will rejoice in the LORD, I will joy in the God of my salvation"* (Habakkuk 3:17-18).

Winston Churchill said, **"A pessimist sees the difficulties in every opportunity. An optimist sees the opportunity in every difficulty."**

George Bernard Shaw added, **"Both optimists and pessimists contribute to society. The optimist invents the aeroplane, the pessimist the parachute."**

Max Lerner stressed, **"I am neither an optimist nor a pessimist, but a possibilist."** An optimist will go from breakthrough to breakthrough, leaving the pessimist to observe and analyse what is happening around them.

1 Peter 3:15, *"But sanctify the Lord God in your hearts: and be ready always to give an answer to every man that asketh you a reason of the hope that is in you with meekness and fear."*

"One cannot think crooked and walk straight" - THOMAS EDISON

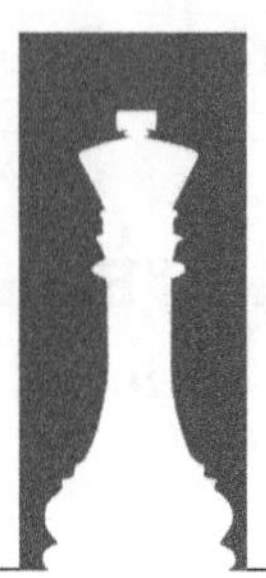

*"It Always Seems
Impossible Until It's Done."*

- Nelson Mandela

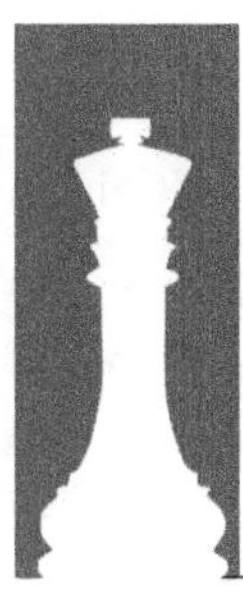

Chapter Three

HABITS OF HIGH ACHIEVERS

WHAT HIGH ACHIEVERS DO:

HIGH ACHIEVERS:

1. Plan while others are playing.

Failing to plan is planning to fail. People don't plan to fail; they fail because they just failed to plan. You don't fail an exam because you don't know anything; no, you fail an exam because you don't know enough. Where you are today spiritually, physically, mentally and financially is because of your planning or failure to plan yesterday and where you will be tomorrow will be based on your planning today or failure to plan.

MEN: As a man and the head or leader of your home, you are the main planner in your family with the help, wisdom and assistance of your wife. Singles in the house, plan and design your life; stop waiting for a life partner. As we saw earlier: Success is not by default; success in life is by design. We can all make a living or we can design a life. An Enviable life. You Choose!

YOU DESIGN YOUR ENLARGEMENT OR YOUR SMALLNESS.

2. Study while others are sleeping.

Pay now, play later; play now, pay later.

Those who learn more earn more. **Your future is not determined by what you earn but by what you learn and what you do with what you learn.**

3. Decide while others are delaying.

Step out while others are idling about. Pursue while others are procrastinating and remember indecision is still a decision. Whether you decide or don't decide, you are deciding. Being decisive is a decision with rewards and Being indecisive is also a decision with consequences. **Choosing not to decide is also a decision.**

4. Prepare while others are daydreaming or procrastinating.

Remember: When preparation meets opportunity, success is inevitable. **Prepare even when there are no opportunities. What you prepare for when there are no opportunities is what will determine what happens to you when opportunities arise.**

Success is where preparation and opportunity meet. Success occurs when preparation and opportunity meet. When preparation meets opportunity, success is inevitable. Prepare in the dark what you will do in the light. (John 9:4; 4:34; Proverbs 12.24, *"The hand of the diligent shall bear rule: but the slothful shall be under tribute."*

DON'T FORGET IN THE DARK WHAT GOD TOLD YOU IN THE LIGHT!

5. Begin while others are stalling or stagnant.

The word stall is to: Stop or cause to stop making progress.

Procrastination is the thief of destiny.

6. Work while others are wishing and waiting for time and chance remembering that those who wait, waste.

There are those who procrastinate by using this slogan: TIME WILL TELL. Time only tells what you tell it or program it to tell by your inputs or investments using time. Time by itself changes nothing. Everything left to time stays the same. A little hard work never goes out of fashion.

America's first billionaire, John D. Rockefeller said: "When work or hard work goes out of fashion, civilisation will totter and fall."

When your hands are folded, your destiny will be folded as well. THE EQUATION FOR ACHIEVERS IS: Your work first then your house.

You are not entitled to build a house without first building your work as King Solomon advised in Proverbs 24:27, *"Prepare thy work without, and make it fit for thyself in the field; and afterwards build thine house."*

PROCESS: You start out in life by working for others (apprenticeship), then work for yourself (based on how faithful you were on another man's job [Luke 16:12] and then eventually work for posterity. [Proverbs 13:22]

Your future starts after 5pm as you work for others during the day developing your skills. It was Zig Ziglar who said: "When you change your attitude about your job, it will make a dramatic difference about your performance on the job."

And Aristotle said, "Pleasure in the job puts perfection in the work."

IS YOUR HEART IN YOUR MINISTRY, YOUR CHURCH, YOUR WORKPLACE, HOME, FAMILY and DOES IT SHOW IN HOW HARD YOU WORK, THE RESULTS YOU PRODUCE, HOW MANY PEOPLE YOU INTRODUCE THERE AND BRING THERE? Each year is a year of working harder and smarter and giving your best to your church and on another man's job to determine when you are entrusted with yours (Luke 16).

7. Think while others are worrying.

Worrying is the art of using your mind to magnify problems while thinking is the art of using your mind to generate and solve problems!

What is your poverty-exit plan and Brexit exit plan for those of us living in the UK? Are you worrying about it or thinking your way through it or out of it? The same mind you are using to engage in the unproductive art or act of worrying, you can use the same mind to do something productive by thinking instead to generate answers.

8. Create or make Room to accommodate the enlargement you are expecting while others are wishing.

Isaiah 54:2-3, *"Enlarge the place of your tent, stretch your tent curtains wide, do not hold back; lengthen your chords, strengthen your stakes. For you will spread out to the right hand and to the left."*

9. Reinvent yourself while others stay the same.

In the year 1965, a young man named Tom graduated from college with a degree in English.

He took a job with an insurance company in Connecticut. After working there for seven years, he transitioned to a new role in the industry and started working for an insurance agency for the next eight years. He was beginning to feel an internal pull to follow his passion. He had always wanted to write a novel. He spent more time away from work working on the novel. His wife recalled Tom's early writing years by saying, He was writing at home every weekend. I told him he should go back to selling insurance. In 1984, after working for almost 20 years in the insurance industry, Tom Clancy finally published his first book, "The Hunt for Red October." He hoped to sell 5,000 copies but by the end of the decade it had sold more than 2 million. Tom Clancy reinvented himself just by writing a novel. You can reinvent yourself too.

10. Save while others are wasting.

Foolish people waste money, average people spend money but wise people invest money. Even though Time is the currency of life, foolish people waste time, average people spend time but wise people invest time. That's what determines those who end up enlarged and those who end up small. As the saying goes: When the tide is out, you will know those who swam naked.

Foolish people believe in luck but wise people believe in the law of cause and effect. Wise people know that a meaningful, significant, impactful and relevant life is determined by choice, not by chance!

11. Invest while others are on a spending spree.

As we saw earlier Foolish people waste time and money, average people spend time and money but wise people invest time and money. What you want more of, invest heavily in it. What you focus more on, is what grows in your heart, in your hands and in Your life. [Galatians 6:6-10]

12. Listen while others are talking.

You learn more by listening than speaking.

God gave us mouths that close and ears that don't; that should tell us something.

The Creator, God, gave us one mouth and two ears; that should also tell us something.

We have two ears and one tongue so that we will listen more and talk less. The quieter you become, the more you can hear. Wisdom is the reward you get for a lifetime of listening when you would have preferred to talk.

ADVISE: SPEAK in such a way that others love to LISTEN to you; LISTEN in such a way that others love to SPEAK to you.

Lesson: Speak less and listen more; you will learn more that way.

SILENCE IS THE BEST REPLY TO A FOOL! Because, Silence is also an answer and silence cannot be misquoted!

When you meet high achievers with proofs i.e. those who know more and have achieved or accomplished more than you in their field, listen more than talk and when given the opportunity, ask sensible, wise and well-prepared questions and then take notes. What you don't respect you don't attract. Trying to claim equality with someone who knows more than you is 'stupidity gone to sea'.

As Albert Einstein said, "The definition of insanity is doing the same thing over and over again, but expecting different results".

13. ARE ADVENTUROUS, EXPECT GREAT THINGS AND ATTEMPT GREAT THINGS WHILE OTHERS ARE OVER CAREFUL, SIT IDLE OR THINK SMALL

Luke 12:32, NLT, *"So don't be afraid, little flock. For it gives your Father great happiness to give you the Kingdom."*

WILLIAM CAREY, THE FATHER OF MODERN MISSIONS PART 1

*7 SECRET LANDING IN INDIA

"Father, wait up!" called eight-year-old Felix Carey as he ran along the upper deck of the ship. "Mother won't do it. After all she's gone through on this journey, she says that climbing overboard and getting into that little fishing boat is just the last straw!"

William Carey turned and laid a hand on his son's shoulder. "Don't worry, Felix. I know Mother is scared, but I'll help her." Felix gazed down at the fishing boat bobbing in the waves. He knew missionaries could not officially enter India and were not welcome here. But he still had concerns.

"Father, what if I slip off the ladder and fall in the water?" asked Felix.

William smiled down at his son. "Do you remember the stories about Captain Cook?

Felix brightened. "Of course I do!"

"Well, think of this as an adventure from Captain Cook's journals, only we're not going just to explore. We're here to share the Gospel with the people of India. God has called us here!"

"Yes, I know," replied Felix triumphantly. **"Expect great things from God! Attempt great things for God!"**

"I didn't know you listened so closely to my sermons!" said William with a twinkle in his eye. "You call your brothers and I'll speak with Mother. Before long, we'll be on Indian soil! And we'll see what great things God will do!"

WHO'S THE STRANGER HERE?

The Indian fishermen put down their nets to watch the spectacle which unfolded as the light-skinned family unloaded their belongings from a fishing boat. "Why are they all staring at us?" Felix asked as he stepped onto the shore in Calcutta.

"We look as strange to them as they do to us!" his father explained. All eyes followed the family as they made their way through the town. The smell of fish was heavy in the air, but soon other smells greeted them. Indian spices, like curry, garlic, and ginger, wafted over from the outdoor market. Indian women dressed in bright colours paused from their shopping to stare, while the children giggled and pointed at the foreigners.

"See all those people?" asked William. "They all need to learn about Jesus!" It was November 11, 1793, and these pioneer English missionaries to India had no idea of the troubles they would face.

WAITING FOR GREAT THINGS

Several months later, William sat on Felix's sleeping mat and stroked his son's forehead. Felix held his knees tightly to his stomach, groaning with the familiar pain.

"Feeling any better, son?"

"I think so, Father," Felix whispered. "I don't want to wait any longer." Felix just wanted to get away from the horrible slum, even if he had to travel while sick.

"Father, why isn't God doing any great things in India yet?"

Felix's words cut to William's heart. He understood the question perfectly. They lived in horrible conditions with little to eat and were often sick with dysentery. William worked long hours to learn the language, and even preached a little, yet no one seemed to care about the Gospel. Was this what God intended for them in India?

"I know how you feel, Felix, but we must be patient. God is with us no matter what, and surely that is a great thing."

The Careys moved not once, but five times during their first seven months in India. Finally, they settled in the town of Mudnabatti, where William found work running a factory. This helped to provide money for their family, but their struggles with illness were far from over.

FATHER, DON'T YOU CARE?

"Father, how can you keep working after all that's happened?" Felix asked late in 1794. "Baby Peter died and Mother won't come out of her room, yet you keep working. It's like you don't even care!"

William looked up from his writing and rubbed his tired eyes. "Felix, I miss Peter as much as anyone. It is a terrible thing to lose a child so young. I pass my days as if in the valley of the shadow of death, but I must go on. He who has called us will be faithful."

Angry tears streamed down Felix's face. "God doesn't seem too faithful to me, Father. The Indians don't want to hear about our God. They have enough gods of their own. Not even one of them has believed. And now mother is sick and Peter is dead! We came here expecting great things, but God has let us down."

"Oh, Felix, God is still here. We must press on and trust Him, even when times are so hard."

William labored on for six years with little encouragement and little support before things began to improve.

HELP ARRIVES

"Those Carey children just run wild," said Hannah Marshman. Hannah and her husband, Joshua, had recently come to India along with William Ward and five others. The eight new missionaries arrived in 1799 to help William.

"William has worked so hard for six years, with his wife sick in bed and no one to help him. It appears the children have picked up some bad habits," answered Joshua. "Perhaps we can help."

Hannah and Joshua did just that. Along with William Ward, they helped William Carey run the mission, open schools, and print the Scriptures. Hundreds of people came to listen when William preached, yet still there were no converts to Christianity. In 1800, the team moved to Serampore, 17 miles north of Calcutta. Before long there was a breakthrough.

GREAT THINGS AT LAST

On December 28, 1800, the missionaries gathered together to walk with Krishna Pal to the river for the big event. Crowds of Hindus yelled and threw rocks to stop Krishna Pal from going through with his plans, but he was determined.

Felix walked alongside William. "Father, Krishna Pal is brave to be baptized when he knows his whole community will reject him and he'll lose his place in society."

"Yes, after seven long years, we can rejoice in the first Indian convert. God has done a great thing!"

"God has done another great thing, Father," said Felix. "My faith has grown stronger as I've talked with Krishna Pal. I want to be baptized today as well."

"Son, I will baptize you with joy!" said William. "This is only the beginning of the great things God will do here in India."

Felix Carey and Krishna Pal both went on to help spread the Gospel in India. William Carey worked in India for 34 more years, the rest of his life. He continued to face many obstacles and trials, but never gave up. Eventually hundreds of Indians came to <u>Christ</u> through William's work. But perhaps his greatest accomplishment was in helping to show people that the Gospel is meant for all races of people all over the world. His example has inspired generations of missionaries to leave the comforts of home and bring the Gospel to those who've never heard it. William truly is the "Father of Modern Missions."

Make It Real! Questions to make you dig a little deeper and think a little harder.

1. Do you think going to another land would be an adventure? Where would you most like to go?

2. People of William Carey's day did not understand that the Gospel is meant for all the people of the world. How do you think William Carey convinced them it is? See Matthew 28:19-20.

3. William Carey pressed on even when it seemed God was distant. Why might that be hard to do?

4. One of the struggles William faced was that he had very little contact with the people from his home in England. Would that be hard for you? Can you write a letter of news and encouragement to a missionary?

Suggested Reading:

- *William Carey: Obliged to Go* by Janet & Geoff Benge (Christian Heroes: Then and Now series), YWAM

- *William Carey: Bearer of Good News* by Renee Taft Meloche (Heroes for Young Readers), YWAM

14. They are people of vision who risk all to make those in their lives great while others are self-absorbed.

I want my husband to be like Ben Carson.

I want my husband to be like Fela Durotoye.

I want my husband to be like Myles Munroe.

I want my husband to be like Robert Kiyosaki.

I want my husband to be like Sam Adeyemi.

I want my husband to be like Enoch Adeboye.

I want my husband to be like Yemi Osinbajo.

I want my husband to be like Steve Harris.

I want my husband to be like Mike Bamiloye.

I want my husband to be like Barak Obama.

I want my husband to be like Olu Jacobs.

I want my husband to be like Voke Roy Onakpoya.

I want my husband to be like DK Olukoya.

I want my husband to be like Bisi Adewale.

I want my husband to be like Praise Fowowe.

I want my husband to be like Joshua Selman Nimmak.

I want my husband to be like Olufukeji Ejimi Adegbeye.

I want my husband to be like Bishop David Oyedepo.

I want my husband to be like Samuel Olagbenjo.

Sister, ...their wives are indeed fortunate to have them.

Hey! Come on. 'Wake up...

Their wives didn't marry the men you know

They built them...

Their wives didn't marry the fire

They fanned the smoke to flame.

Their wives didn't marry the celebrities

They took a chance on the nonentities.

Their wives didn't marry the glory

They were part of the stories.

Never give up on a man with a vision...

To them belong the future.

#celebrating_the_women_who_risked_all_for_their_men.

God bless your home!'

- Felix Adejumo

15. They persist while others quit.

The great basketball player, Michael Jordan once said, "I've missed more than 9,000 times in my career. I've lost almost 300 games. 26 times I've been trusted to take the game winning shot and missed. I've failed over and over and over again in my life. And that is why I succeed."

Persist while others are quitting.

Remember: Winners don't quit and quitters don't win.

That's why Winston Churchill said: "Never, never, never give up."

Other MOTIVATING QUOTES FOR ACHIEVERS:

I.   He conquers who endures.

II.   You are not a failure until you quit.

III.   Fall seven times stand up eight. - Japanese proverb

IV.   When the world says, 'Give up', hope whispers "Try it one more time." - Author unknown

V.   Adversity causes some to break and others to break records. - William Ward

16. They are selfless and committed price-payers for what they desire while others keep wishing

A missionary society wrote to David Livingstone and asked, "Have you found a good road to where you are? If so, we want to know how to send other men to join you." Livingstone wrote back, "If you have men who will come only if they know there is a good road, I don't want them. I want men who will come if there is no road at all." – Unknown Source

Many people like to be involved in something but will not commit to it. Commitment means to be dedicated and devoted to something no matter what. Commitment is an 'If I perish, I perish' attitude. It takes courage to commit; it takes loyalty and faithfulness to stick with a person, an organization or a movement. The bible says, *"And let us not be weary in well doing: for in due season we shall reap, if we faint not"* (Galatians 6:9). It takes desire, laser-like focus, determination, decisiveness, dedication, discipline, death to self, diligence and toughness of heart to see through a personal dream. We need sacrifice and discipline to keep going when the going gets tough.

17. Smile while others are frowning.

Habakkuk 3:17-19, **"Though the fig tree does not bud and there are no grapes on the vines, though the olive crop fails and the fields produce no food, though there are no sheep**

in the pen and no cattle in the stalls, <u>yet I will rejoice in the LORD, I will be joyful in God my Savior.</u> The Sovereign LORD is my strength; he makes my feet like the feet of a deer, he enables me to tread on the heights. [TO WALK IN MINE HIGH PLACES] For the director of music. On my stringed instruments."

YET I WILL REJOICE! SO, JOY IS A CHOICE YOU MAKE IN THE FACE OF NOTHING WORKING, NOT A GIFT YOU CLAIM.

Jane Lane said: "Of all the things you wear, your expression is the most important."

Isaiah 12:3, *"Therefore, with joy shall ye draw water out of the wells of salvation."*

Proverbs 17:22, *"A merry heart maketh good like medicine but a broken spirit drieth the bones..."*

18. Commend while others are criticising.

Use your mouth for profitable ventures.

19. Pray while others are playing, prying (being busybodies) and becoming a prey.

The word Prey means Hunted to be destroyed due to their own negligence of duty, laziness, idleness and slothfulness or irresponsibility while consumed with self aggrandisement. Be warfare conscious. The magnitude of what God wants to use you for dictates the attacks you face.

20. Keep Tithing, Giving and Serving while others are hoarding, keeping, hiding and withholding. *5

Remain GENEROUS.

Proverbs 11:24, *"There is that scattereth and yet increaseth and there is that holdeth more than is meet but it leads to poverty."*

When you come into ENLARGEMENT, remember and never forget where God picked you from while others are choosing to forget and suffering from deliberate self-imposed Alzheimer's, amnesia and dementia.

*REMEMBER HOW YOU GOT THERE AND STAY HUMBLE AND still IN SERVICE.

When you become a high achiever, **Don't RAISE your standard of living; rather, raise Your STANDARD OF GIVING.**

*GOD IS THE ULTIMATE AUTHOR OF SUCCESS, ENLARGEMENT, ACHIEVEMENT AND ACCOMPLISHMENT.

Never forget God who made you and those who helped you along the way to become who you are or become including your Pastor, your church and the strategic people [Psalm 137:5-6; Deuteronomy 8:17-18]

Psalms 18:19, *"He brought me forth also into a large place; he delivered me, because he delighted in me."*

Psalms 18:36, *"Thou hast enlarged my steps under me, that my feet did not slip."*

21. Show people you care while others don't.

To become an achiever, involves people. So, STARTING from TODAY, SHOW THAT YOU CARE FOR PEOPLE! SHOW PEOPLE YOU CARE! People can tell whether you truly care for them or are using them as a means to an end. Let people feel you love and care for them genuinely and are not just out for what to get from them. Empower people! How can you show obvious disinterest in what someone is saying or doing and claim you are interested in them or in what they are doing including church? Ask yourself questions like 'Am I growing spiritually or mentally? Why? Because, you can't give what you don't have. Who am I adding value to daily and weekly? Who can point at me and say that apart from God, I am also the reason their life is better than it was before? SHARE YOUR GOD, YOUR KNOWLEDGE, WISDOM AND FAILURE AND SUCCESS EXPERIENCES WITH OTHERS; that's how you become an achiever.

*Remember: Success without a successor is failure! Succeeding alone is failure! YOU ARE NOT SUCCESSFUL UNTIL YOU HELP OTHERS SUCCEED. SUCCESSFUL PEOPLE DON'T REACH THEIR GOALS ALONE - THEY teach, train and HELP OTHERS BECOME ACHIEVERS!

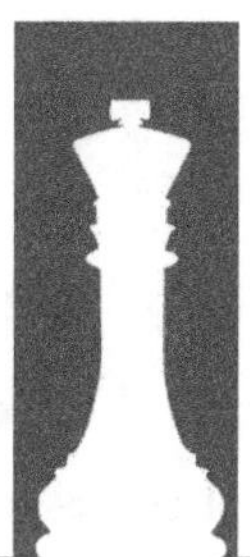

"Rich People Stay Rich By Living Like They Are Broke. Broke People Stay Broke By Living Like They're Rich!"

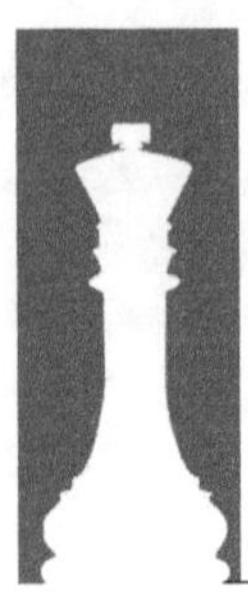

Chapter Four

WHAT SEPARATES THE RICH FROM THE POOR?

What separates the rich from the poor is their Choices in life. LIFE Is about choices. Choices determine decisions; right choices lead to good decisions and wrong choices lead to bad decisions. Every road has a destination and He who chooses the beginning of a road also chooses its outcome and destination.

The rich make themselves rich by what they do and don't do; surprisingly the poor also make themselves poor by what they do and don't do which they must do.

Proverbs 22:13, *"The slothful man saith, There is a lion without, I shall be slain in the streets."*

He made a choice so ended up poor.

1. Rich people choose the thoughts they wish to think; poor people allow others to give them thoughts to think...

2. Rich people see, plan and prepare ahead for 3 or 4 generations while poor people plan for Saturday night. They can't see

beyond their nose i.e. Their immediate environment and state.

"A good man (woman) leaveth an inheritance to his children's children; (grandchildren) and the wealth of the sinner is laid up for the righteous." - Proverbs 13:22 ASV

You must Build with generations in mind not just for today.

The least we are expected from the scriptures to prepare and plan for is for our grandchildren not just our children.

Live today with tomorrow clearly in mind. It will dictate and determine your choices and decisions in life.

Failure to plan is planning to fail.

With a building generationally-mindset, you leave legacies behind like The Rockefeller Foundation, Hilton, Ford empires, Microsoft, Apple, Google, Facebook, YouTube, Twitter, ORU, Spurgeons, etc.

3. Poor people get all they can, can all they get and sit on the can; Rich people get all they can, open the can up by investing and redistributing what's in the can to add value to others.

4. Rich people invest heavily in themselves and into others; Poor people don't pour anything into themselves so have nothing or not much to pour into others.

5. Poor people give excuses for why they are who, what, how, where they are; they always play the victim and blame game blaming everyone else but themselves for their plight and condition while Rich people find reasons to move forward and succeed.

6. Poor people hoard the little they have out of fear of tomorrow; rich people give and invest the little they have to create their tomorrow.

7. Rich people take risks; the poor are fearful of what if? Fearful of failure, people's opinion, rain, weather, imaginary lions. "The slothful says saith, *There is* a lion in the way; a lion *is* in the streets. (Proverbs 26:13)

    **The riskiest risk is not taking risks.

8. Rich people are always engaged in personal development, ever learning and improving themselves; poor people don't. Some are content with where they are waiting for handouts.

9. Rich people defy the status quo, break records, set new records and new standards; the poor settle for what is and even argue against the status quo.

    Poverty can be inherited but it's a choice to stay in poverty or to get out of it.

TO BE BORN INTO A POOR FAMILY IS EXCUSABLE BUT TO LEAVE THAT FAMILY POOR IS INEXCUSABLE!

10. The poor have entitlement mentality while the rich have taking responsibility mentality.

11. The rich build generationally I.e. With generations and posterity in mind but the poor build in their stomach with only today in mind i.e. let's eat and drink for tomorrow we die.

12. Rich people use their head before their feet and hand. Poor people use only their feet. What puts you ahead in life is more your head than your feet and hands.

13. The rich have this mentality: Riches is what you have but wealth is who you are. To the poor it's vice versa. Rich is what they want to be and wealth is what they want to have. Rich people are first of all wealthy in their minds before they are in their pockets.

14. Poor people are lazy; the rich are diligent. Rich people are addicted to information and continually stay informed; poor people stay ignorant. [Proverbs 22:29; 18:16; 17:8]

15. Poor people lack creativity; the rich are creative, innovative and inventive. Rich and great minds discuss ideas, average minds discuss events and small or poor minds discuss people (gossip, etc.).

16. Rich people use their minds to think to generate ideas to create wealth; poor people use their mind to worry and their mouth to complain and blame everyone else.

17. Poor people task their hand more while the rich task their brains more.

18. Poor people are Procrastinators while Rich people are Proactive.

19. The poor engage in work that demands more of effort while the rich engage in work that demands more of wisdom.

20. The rich are givers and generous while the poor are stingy. Isaac sowed in that land and in the same year reaped a hundred fold in Genesis 26; "Blessed are ye that sow beside all waters, that send forth thither the feet of the ox and the ass." - Isaiah 32:20

21. The poor don't like hard work; some actually hate and detest the word 'work' but the rich love their work, smart work and get better at it every day. They consider their vocation as a vacation. [Proverbs 22:29]

22. Poor people give excuses for being or staying poor; Rich people find reasons to become rich and wealthy. [Proverbs 22:29]

Numbers 13:30, *"And Caleb stilled the people before Moses, and said, Let us go up at once, and possess it; for we are well able to overcome it."*

23. The poor can't see anything much more success while the rich can see potential, possibilities, progress and success. Helen Keller a blind woman from birth who succeeded in life was asked what was worse than blind eyes. Her answer was classic: ONE WITH SIGHT BUT NO VISION!!

24. Mike Murdock said the hatred of the rich by the poor could be the reason why they are still poor.

25. **RICH PEOPLE STAY RICH BY LIVING LIKE THEY ARE BROKE. BROKE PEOPLE STAY BROKE BY LIVING LIKE THEY'RE RICH!**

References

*1   Refer to my book SUCCESS HAS NO UNCLES
www.houseofjudah.org.uk

*2   Refer to my book, 21 LIONS YOU MUST KILL
www.houseofjudah.org.uk

*3   21 LIONS YOU MUST KILL www.houseofjudah.org.uk

*4   Truthbook.com

*5   Get a copy of my books Releasing the power of First fruit offerings and Tithes and 50 Direct and Indirect Implications of not tithing or giving purposefully

*6   7 things successful people do that they will not tell you
*** mine

*7   https://en.m.wikipedia.org.wiki William Carey

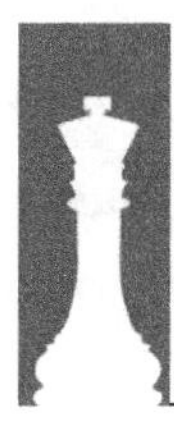

The Greatest Gift

If you want to take advantage of the contents of this message by asking God to give you power to lead, from which Adam fell, you need to give your life to Jesus Christ. If you have never met or experienced a definite encounter with Jesus Christ, you can know Him today. You can make your life right with Him by accepting Him as your personal Lord and Saviour by praying the following prayer out loud where you are. Pray this prayer with me now:

PRAYER FOR SALVATION:

"O God, I ask you to forgive me for my sins. I believe You sent Jesus to die on the cross for me and confess it with my mouth. I receive Jesus Christ as my personal Lord and Saviour and confess Him as Lord of my life and I give my life willingly to Him now. Thank you Lord for saving me and for making me a new person in Jesus' Name, (2 Corinthians 5:17) Amen."

If you prayed this prayer, you have now become a child of God (John 1:12) and I welcome you to the family of God. Please let me know about your decision for Jesus by writing to me.

I would like to send you some free literature to help you in your new walk with the Lord. So, send me an email @ info@ houseofjudah.org.uk or bishopmhw@gmail.com.

Or Call (within the UK):
0208 689 6010 / 07956 815 714

Outside the UK:
+44 208 689 6010
+44 7956 815 714

Or visit us at:
www.houseofjudah.org.uk
michaelhutton-wood.org

Alternatively Email us at:
info@houseofjudah.org.uk
bishopmhw@gmail.com

Other Books & Leadership Manuals By Author

1.   A Must For Every New Convert

2.   You Need To Do The Ridiculous In Order To Experience The Miraculous

3.   175 Reasons Why You Cannot And Will Not Fail In Life

4.   What To Do In The Darkest Hour Of Your Trial [125 Bible Truths You Must Know, Believe, Remember, Confess And Do]

5.   Why You should Pray And How You should Pray For Your Pastor and Your Church Daily

6.   200 Questions You Must Ask, Investigate And Know Before You Say 'I Do'

7.   I Shall Rise Again

8.   How to negotiate your desired future with today's currency

9.   Leadership Secrets

10. Leadership Nuggets

11. Leadership Capsules

12. What Is Ministry?

Training Manuals For Impactful Leadership & Effective Ministry

- Academy 101 [House Of Judah Academy Curriculum]
- Ministry 101
- Leadership 101
- Pastoral Leadership 101 From School Of Impactful Pastoral Leadership

To order copies of any of these books, ministry or leadership manuals or for a product catalog of other literature, and CDs, DVDs, write to:

Michael Hutton-Wood Ministries
1st Floor, 387 London Road, Croydon. CR0 3PB.
UK.

OR [in the UK call]   **0208 689 6010**
    [outside UK call] **+ 44 208 6896010**

You can also place your order online as you visit our website:
www.houseofjudah.org.uk

You can email us at:
info@houseofjudah.org.uk
michaelhuttonwood@gmail.com

Global Initiatives & Ministries Within The Ministry

TV MINISTRY IN THE UK

Watch Leadership Secrets on:
KICC TV SKY Channel 590
Tuesday – 3.00pm
Saturday – 5.30pm

Watch Us On:
YouTube
Subscribe to the JUDAH PRAISE NETWORK and
LIVESTREAMING @ www.houseofjudah.org.uk

Follow Bishop Hutton-Wood on Facebook, Whatsapp,
Youtube, Twitter, Instagram, Soundcloud, and Download
Bishop's App

# Partnering With A Global Ministry Within A Ministry

Michael Hutton-Wood Ministries (The HUTTON-WOOD WORLD OUTREACH MINISTRY) is the apostolic, missions, world outreach, and evangelistic wing of the House of Judah (Praise) Ministries with a mission to God's end time church and the nations of the earth.

This ministry was born out of a strong God-given mandate to reach, touch and impact the nations of the earth with the gospel of Christ and bring back divine order, discipline, integrity, godly character, excellence and stability to God's people and God's house. It has a strong apostolic mandate to set in order the things that are out of order and lacking in the church [The Body of Christ] – (Titus 1:5).

Its mission is to save the lost at any cost, depopulate hell and populate heaven with souls that have experienced in full, the new birth, renewal of mind, to produce believers walking in the fullness of their Godly inheritance, divine health, prosperity and authority to take their homes, communities, cities and nations for Christ and occupy till Christ returns. It is to raise a people without spot, wrinkle or blemish. The man of God's passion and drive is that as truly as he lives, this earth shall be filled with the knowledge of the glory of the Lord as the waters cover the sea.

His determination is not to rest, hold back or keep silent until he sees the body of Christ established as a praise in the earth. (Numbers 14:21; Habakkuk 2:14; Isaiah 62:6-7)

If you would like to join the faithful brethren and partners of this great ministry by becoming a partner as we believe God for ten thousand partners to partner with this vision prayerfully and financially, **you can GIVE ONLINE at www.houseofjudah.org. uk.**

Call:

+44 [0] 208 689 6010 for more details.

Philippians 4:19 be your portion and experience as you partner with this work and global mandate. Shalom!

Generational Leadership Training Institute
[The Leaders' Factory]

The Mandate: Raising Generational Leaders, Impacting Nations.

The Generational Leadership Training Institute (GLTI) is the Leadership training and mentoring wing of our ministry with a global mandate to raise leaders with a generational thinking mindset, not a now mentality and to fulfil the Law of Explosive Growth – To add growth, lead followers – To multiply, lead leaders.

This is a Bible College, Leadership Training Institute fulfilling the Matthew 9:37-38 mandate of developing and releasing labourers for the end time harvest. We offer fulltime and part time certificate, diploma, degree and short twelve-week courses in biblical studies, counselling, leadership, practical ministry and schools of prosperity. Its aim is to raise leaders who know and live not just by the anointing but by ministerial ethics, leaders who build with a long term mentality, who live today with tomorrow in mind. The mission of this unique educational and impartation institution is to transform followers into generational leaders and its motto is to raise leaders of discipline, integrity, godly character and excellence - D.I.C.E.

For correspondence, full time, part time, online courses, prospectus, fees and registration forms for the next course, call

0208 689 6010 or write to the Registrar, GLTI, 1st Floor, 387 London Road, Croydon. CR0 3PB. UK or from outside UK call +44 208 689 6010.

Additional information can be obtained from visiting our website www.houseofjudah.org.uk looking for THE LEADERS FACTORY.

This is a hutton-wood publication

LEADERS FACTORY INTERNATIONAL

MANDATE: 'In the business of training, developing and raising and releasing more leaders and leaders of leaders.'

'Leaders must be close enough to relate to others, but far enough ahead to motivate them.' – John Maxwell

'You must live with people to know their problems, and live with God in order to solve them.' – P. T. Forsyth

If you, your organisation, college, university, business or church would like to invite Dr. Michael Hutton-Wood for a Motivational-speaking, mentoring or leadership coaching engagement or to organize or hold a Leaders Factory seminar or conference, Leadership Development or Human Capital building seminar, Emerging leaders seminar, Management seminar, Business seminar, Effective people-management, Wealth-creation seminar or training for your workers, leaders, staff, ministers, employers, employees, congregation, youth, etc. you can contact us on 0208 689 6010 [UK] +44208 689 6010 [OUTSIDE UK].

Alternatively by email at:

- info@houseofjudah.org.uk

- bishopmhw@gmail.com

- leadersfactoryinternational@yahoo.com

VISIT our website: www.houseofjudah.org.uk
                 or michaelhutton-wood.org

MANDATE:

Releasing Potential - Maximizing Destiny
Raising Generational Leaders - Impacting Nations

SIMPA:
Sceptre International Ministers & Pastors Association

This covenant mandate comes from Genesis 49:10: 'The sceptre [of Leadership] shall not depart from JUDAH, nor a lawgiver from between his feet, until Shiloh come and unto Him shall the gathering of the people be'

Other covenant scriptures backing this mandate are: Isaiah 55:4 & Titus 1:5. We have a leadership assignment to RAISE GENERATIONAL LEADERS TO IMPACT NATIONS BY DISCOVERING MEN/WOMEN AND EMPOWERING THEM TO RELEASE THEIR POTENTIAL TO MAXIMIZE THEIR DESTINY.

SIMPA is a multi-cultural fellowship/network of diverse Christian leaders, pastors and ministers that recognize the need for fathering, covering and mentoring. The heartbeat of the man of God is to pour into the willing and obedient what has made him and keeps making him from what he's learnt from his father in the Lord, his teachers and mentors which is working for him and producing maximally. He said: 'I discovered this secret early: Not to learn from or follow those who make promises but from those who have obtained the promises, proofs and results.

REMEMBER: YOU DON'T NEED TO MAKE NOISE TO MAKE NEWS.

SO: FOLLOW NEWS-MAKERS NOT NOISE-MAKERS!'

These are a few of the mindsets of the man of God:

- When the students are ready, the teacher will teach.

- 'YOU NEED FATHERS TO FATHER YOU TO GROW FEATHERS TO FLY.' – Bishop Oyedepo

- 'Without a father to father you, you can never grow feathers to fly and go further in life, than they went and accomplish more than they did.' – Michael Hutton-Wood

- Don't raise money; raise men and you'll have all the money you need to accomplish your assignment.

- There is no new thing under the sun – King Solomon

- What you desire to attain, become and accomplish in life, someone has accomplished it – find them, follow them, learn from them, sow into them and their resource materials and you will do more than they did and get there faster.

- Teachers, Trainers, Mentors and Fathers give you speed/ acceleration in every field of endeavour.

- Isaac Newton is known to have said the following:

- 'If I have seen further it has been by standing on the shoulders of those who have gone ahead of me.'

- Variant translations: 'Plato is my friend, Aristotle is my friend, but my best friend is truth.'

- 'Plato is my friend — Aristotle is my friend — truth is a greater friend.'

- 'If I have seen further it is only by standing on the shoulders of giants.'

- Without a reference you can never become a reference.

- If you don't refer to anyone no one will refer to you.

- Who laid / lays hands on you and what did / do they leave behind?

- This is not a money-making venture but rather about covering and empowerment for fulfilment of destiny and assignment within time allocated.

- The goal of SIMPA is to spiritually cover, strengthen, equip, empower, train, mentor and encourage and lift up the arms/ hands of both emerging and active [full and part time] pastors, ministers and leaders and by so doing release them to fulfil their respective assignments both in ministry and the market place.

IF YOU WOULD LIKE TO BE A PART OF SIMPA, ASK FOR A REGISTRATION FORM & PAMPHLET FROM OUR INFORMATION DESK in House of Judah or email: *info@houseofjudah.org.uk* or *michaelhuttonwood@gmail.com*

Or call [in the UK] 0208 689 6010

[Outside UK call] + 44 208 689 6010 requesting for SIMPA registration form and pamphlet.

– SEE YOU ON TOP! Shalom! – Bishop

PARTNERSHIP:

In the UK write or send cheque donations to:
Michael Hutton-Wood Ministries
1st Floor, 387 London Road, Croydon. CR0 3PB

In the UK Call: 0208 689 6010; 07956 815 714

Outside the UK call: +44 208 689 6010; + 44 7956 815 714

Fax: +44 20 8689 3301

Email: info@houseofjudah.org.uk
   bishopmhw@gmail.com
   leadersfactoryinternational@yahoo.com

Or visit or GIVE ONLINE at our secure WEBSITE:
www.houseofjudah.org.uk

HWP
Dr. Michael Hutton-Wood
© 2019

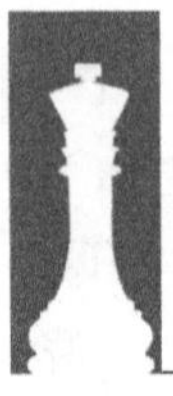

NOTES